❧

For Andrea McFadden and Christopher Woods

Drivin' along, singin' a song, side by side

❧

Acknowledgements

Our thanks go to the following gardeners, garden advisors and editors.
This book would still have been possible without them (with the exception of
Susan Yetter) but we're still mighty glad we had their assistance.

❧

Craig Bergmann and James Grigsby

Bourton House

Beth Chatto

Coton Manor Gardens

Denver Botanic Gardens

Susan Clotfelter

Joan Donner

Fergus Garrett

Kelly Grummons

Norma Hazen

HERBS
in pots

HERBS
in pots

artful and practical herbal containers

**ROB PROCTOR AND
DAVID MACKE**

INTERWEAVE PRESS

Herbs in Pots
Artful and Practical Herbal Containers

Cover design: Bren Frisch
Illustrations by Gayle Ford and Susan Strawn Bailey
Photography copyright 1999 by Rob Proctor, Joe Coca and Interweave Press (cover, pp. 172, 176, 180) and Joseph A. Strauch, Jr. (p. 48)
Illustrations copyright 1999 by Interweave Press
Text copyright 1999 by Rob Proctor and David Macke

 Interweave Press, Inc.
201 East Fourth Street
Loveland, Colorado 80537-5655

Printed in the United States by R.R. Donnelley & Sons Company.

Library of Congress Cataloging-in-Publication Data

Proctor, Rob
  Herbs in pots: a practical guide to container gardening indoors and out/Rob Proctor & David Macke.
    p. cm.
  Includes index.
  ISBN 1-883010-52-7
  1. Herb gardening. 2. Container gardening. I. Macke, David, 1951- . II. title.
  SB351.H5P755 1999
  635'.7—dc21   99-24679
                                                        CIP

First Printing: 7.5M:599:RRD

Dean Howes

Hidcote Manor

Ivy Cottage

Christopher Lloyd

Tom and Diane Peace

Rabbit Shadow Herb Farm

Laura and Tim Spear, Forest Edge Gardens

Lauren Springer

Sticky Wicket

John Tordoff

Ann Weckbaugh

Susan Yetter

TABLE OF CONTENTS

INTRODUCTION

MOST PEOPLE TAKE POTTED PLANTS FOR granted. It's pleasant to idly pass some potted flowers near the elevator, or sip cocktails beneath the fronds of palms and ferns in a favorite watering hole. In time, these folks might find they want a spot of color by the front door, some herbs for snipping in the kitchen window, or a tropical-looking philodendron in a corner of the living room. Impulse buyers become container gardeners almost by accident. A mum speaks to their Thanksgiving spirit, a basket of ivy-leaf geraniums begs to hang from their porch, or a bay tree promises a hundred savory stews. The door swings open.

Growing herbs in pots takes simple, easily mastered skills. Learning how to gauge the right plant for the right pot soon becomes second nature. So does watering, fertilizing, and siting a potted specimen in the optimum exposure. We all learn to trouble shoot, usually spotting a problem before it gets out of hand. We think most gardeners are innately creative, and we don't think most of them feel completely satisfied growing their favorite herbs in a convenient spot near the back door year after year. There's more.

Mastering the practical leads to the artistry. Every musician knows that it takes practice to get to Carnegie Hall. Every gardener knows that it takes time and patience before they're ready to give Rosemary Verey, Marco Polo Stufano, or Lauren Springer a run for the money.

More than time and patience, it takes inspiration. We get ours from the Rosemary's, Marco's, and Lauren's of this world—the many talented, creative gardeners we call friends. We feel compelled to share what we've learned in words and pictures.

Books about container gardening usually don't pay much attention to herbs. The expensive ones feature inspirational pho-

Creativity rules when devising unusual and attractive plant combinations for the container garden.

tographs (shot in lovely English mood lighting) of budget-breaking antique urns spilling with unrealistic expectations. Herb lovers like us often feel a little left out. Or, when herbs are discussed in one of those formula how-to manuals, their planting is treated with about as much passion as one might use to give instructions to install a bathroom shelf. An inordinate amount of ink is devoted to the most minuscule of details, such as ideal potting mixes with recipes that would baffle Julia Child.

We're all for exploring every nuance of growing herbs in pots, but instructing a neophyte gardener to include leaf mold in his or her homemade potting soil mixture strikes us as ludicrous. Most of us want to plant tomorrow or perhaps next weekend, and we don't have time to wait for the leaves to fall, much less turn into mold. In fact, we don't give a hoot about leaf mold. We make compost in a disreputable pile hidden over by the potting shed and add some of it to our potting mix, along with some sand if we've got it, or some extra aquarium gravel. Like cooks who improvise with a pinch of this and a dash of that, we garden by the seat of our pants.

Foliage shapes, sizes, and colors form the foundation of container gardens; this trough of curry plant, ivy, and artemisia remains attractive whether or not plants are in bloom.

If it weren't so conformist, we would display a bumper sticker reading "Question authority." That's not to say that we don't believe in using common sense or having opinions. Successful container gardening is built on understanding not only what plants need, but what we, as gardeners, can offer them. From one part of the country to another, that varies. We can't all grow a particular plant in the same way; sometimes we have to face the fact that we can't grow a plant at all. But that's rare.

Herb gardening has so many facets that there's room for everybody. There's the culinary herb, of course. Everybody eats; it might as well be fun and creative. Herbs have entered the mainstream kitchen and patio. If we're going to use them, we might as well grow them in creative ways. And we might as well swap a few recipes, although we might point out that our "pinch of this" style should be kept in mind.

We'll give a frank assessment of the ups and downs of growing herbs indoors. There's always plenty to do indoors, including planting seeds, striking cuttings, and fighting whiteflies.

Passionate gardeners find outlets for their creativity. Many get carried away with

RULES?

Just for the record, we don't follow rules, and we don't write them. Rules only apply under controlled circumstances—a garden doesn't qualify.

topiary, what our publisher Linda Ligon labels "the ultimate herbal pet." Lacking feline or canine companionship, we too have found ourselves happy to keep a few herbal pets around. Some of our friends have enough to start a whole herbal kennel.

Other herbal pursuits include window-box gardening (an art form all to itself) and hanging gardens, which we're tempted to say take container gardening to new heights, but we won't. Some people concentrate their efforts on miniature gardens. These are fascinating forays into a special Lilliputian world populated by the borrowers, Thumbelina, and life-sized people with very nimble fingers.

Scent is another captivating side of growing herbs in containers. Any patio or balcony can harbor great-smelling plants that may be put to use in the kitchen or household or simply enjoyed for the moment. The Victorians were great fans of herbs for scent. In the days before wall-mounted and plug-in scent dispensers, kitchen exhaust fans, and concern about smoking cigars around children, pleasant scents were prized wherever they could be found. Gardeners embraced scented geraniums, which quickly became fixtures in

Keeping plants in containers allows those with widely varying cultivation requirements to cozy up together.

many households. In keeping with the Victorian penchant for clutter, they were kept where ladies' long skirts could brush them as they passed. We keep our scented geraniums on our back porch over the winter and often rub their leaves on the way out the door. During the summer, we feature them throughout the groupings on our patios. We rarely meet a visitor who can resist a cutting.

Many health-conscious gardeners want to grow healing herbs. We feel uncomfortable talking about herbal remedies, except perhaps for making a soothing chamomile tea or dabbing some aloe on a sting or burn. The subject of herbal healing is beyond our scope. Neither of us has a medical degree, (although Dr. Proctor has a nice ring to it) or experience in herbal therapy. Even if we don't try to treat every ailment with herbs, we do feel healthier just including fresh herbs in our diet all year.

Even if salves and poultices aren't high on your list of priorities, we hope you'll enjoy growing herbs as much as we do. There's truly an herb for every pot and a pot for every situation. For hot and dry situations, desert herbs like aloes and agaves thrive for even the negligent gardener, providing fascinating structures and textures in the process. At the other end of the light spectrum, herbs such as lungworts, rushes, and moneywort grow wonderfully in light shade, although deep shade (such as that cast by an evergreen tree) is unusually challenging. We can offer a few herbs (we really mean a few, so we might as well get it out of the way: sweet woodruff and ivy) that grow passably well in this deep gloom, but perhaps you'll discover a passion for garden sculpture or your blue spruce will become infested by tussock moths, hastening its demise.

Continuing with the many facets of herb gardening for every region and every interest, we'll delve into the hot topic of tropicalismo, which focuses on the tropical and subtropical plants that are now riding a crest of renewed popularity. Also wildly successful at the moment are aquatic herbs such as papyrus, rushes, watercress, and the like that may be easily grown in water pots or small patio-size water features.

While we often discuss possibilities of which herbs thrive in containers, there are others that should be confined in pots to protect the rest of the garden from them. These are the garden thugs that can drive a gardener crazy. They arrive as innocent-looking clumps recently dug by so-called friends, but quickly unleash their terror on their neighbors (and possibly entire neighborhoods). These naughty herbs get the "Go Directly to Jail" card from us, where they can be safely enjoyed.

There's more to growing herbs in pots than just the nuts and bolts. It's the uninhibited use of them that we find so exciting.

We don't treat all our plants so rudely. In fact, we're often quite nice to them, such as when we give our houseplants an invigorating summer vacation. Truth be told, it diminishes our summer chores by getting the dusty things out of the house, but many of them respond beautifully and reveal ornamental qualities that we tend to forget during our long-term relationships with them.

There's more to growing herbs in pots than just the nuts and bolts. It's the uninhibited use of them that we find so exciting and satisfying. Start, as we do, with a single, bold specimen in a handsome pot and build from there. Learn to make wonderful combinations of herbs (and other fascinating plants that mingle with them artfully) that highlight their textures, forms, and flowers.

One pot leads to more. Grouping them to best effect becomes an art in itself, using unifying elements or highlighting the most intriguing plants. These groupings turn a plain patio into a garden or, in some cases, a jungle. For people who love to live outdoors, and to whom sight and scent are vital, we'll offer some examples that might easily be adapted to any situation where there's room for a table and a few chairs.

And if that's not enough, we'll go a step further to suggest that pots of herbs can make grand statements when placed directly in the garden—in borders, along paths, and as centerpieces of beds. You might be surprised to find that an attractive pot and the living plants within serves much better as a focal point than a mass-produced sculpture.

Finally, we'll explore using herbal containers in unique, even quirky ways. Incorporating found elements from the attic or flea market is a time-honored tradition that herb lovers hold dear. Go on, why hold back? Our only fear, aside from seeing the return of cut-and-painted tire planters, is that our nation's thrift stores and flea markets are fast running out of nostalgic items suitable for planting. We're contemplating forming a task force to deal with the problem, but it will have to wait. We've got pots to soak, soil mixes to blend, and plants to harden off. Another season is upon us.

CHAPTER 1
HERBAL KNOW-HOW

ALMOST ANYTHING THAT WILL HOLD SOIL can, and probably has, been used as a container for herbs—teacups, old shoes, tractor tires—but this is not to say that anything that can hold soil should be used. Personality and experience are critical factors in choosing containers for herbs. For outdoor containers, all but the most fastidious, experienced herb growers should begin with at least a 12-inch-diameter container for most plants, with the possible exception of succulents and other dryland specimens. Small containers may require watering more than once a day or an irrigation system, but we'll get to that later.

Containers are made of many materials, and each type has its advantages and drawbacks. A gardener takes a clay pot for granted—a simple object, molded from sticky red earth and fired to brittle hardness. Yet a dusty, bone-dry new pot is just the ticket to a new gardening adventure.

We own more clay pots than most gardeners do—about 600 at last count—because we're nuts about container gardening. There's almost no limit to what we can grow on our patio during the summer. The workhorse of containers is terra-cotta. These pots range in size from smaller than a teacup to more than 3 feet in diameter. They vary from the common, rimmed utility pot to ornately decorated ones. Terra-cotta is available as shallow bulb pots, deeper lemon pots, tall, thin rose pots, and a tremendous variety of fanciful shapes. Gardeners, especially novices, generally get good results when using clay pots for patio containers. By varying the size and adding or removing saucers beneath the pots, you can find terra-cotta containers for every herb you'd ever care to grow.

Clay pots have several advantages: terra-cotta "breathes," allowing air to reach the plants' roots. Evaporating moisture from

Terra-cotta is the workhorse of the container-garden world because it breathes,
but other container materials are useful, too.

the pot surface cools the roots, much as if they were planted in the ground.

Terra-cotta's ability to breathe, however, can be one of its biggest drawbacks. Untreated, the dry red clay wicks water from the soil inside the container, drying the plant's roots. So before planting in terra-cotta containers, soak them in water. Small pots are easily submerged in a sink or a garbage can full of water, but larger containers often require a little more imagination. When the container is completely submerged, you'll see strings of tiny bubbles, much like those in a glass of champagne, rising to the surface. When the bubbles stop, the container is saturated.

Soaking pots can be a bit of a nuisance, but it is well worth the effort. Terra-cotta is so good at wicking water that on hot, dry days it is nearly impossible to pour on enough water to keep the soil moist if the pot itself hasn't been saturated.

At the end of the growing season, terra-cotta pots should be emptied and allowed to dry out. Even when they seem dry, enough moisture may remain to make the pots susceptible to cracking or flaking in

*P*ots that have been neglected for a few days during midsummer will often dry out completely, bringing their inhabitants near death.

freezing weather. We lose several pots each winter—we don't have the storage space to bring them all indoors—but we accept this as part of gardening. Each spring before the new planting, it's a good idea to scrub clay pots and to give them another thorough soaking but, seriously, who has the time?

We're sticklers about watering, but sometimes we miss a pot or two. Pots that have been neglected for a few days during midsummer often will dry out completely, bringing their inhabitants near death. To bring the plants back to life, plunge the pot in a bucket of water to soak the soil and saturate the terra-cotta. Overly dry soil won't absorb water, so returning to the normal watering routine just won't work; the water runs right out the bottom of the pot.

Glazed terra-cotta and ceramic containers are also available in many sizes, shapes, and colors, and for reasonable prices. These richly toned pots add color to container groupings and work well for many plants, although they don't breathe as do unglazed pots. Their nonporous nature, however, makes them ideal as smaller containers and for moisture-loving plants such as primroses or cannas. Those without drainage holes are ideal as cache pots or for water gardening with horsetails, water lilies, watercress, sweet flag, or water mint (*Mentha aquatica*). Glazed containers are seldom frost-proof.

Wooden containers offer many of the advantages of terra-cotta. They are generally lightweight and easily constructed to suit special needs. The biggest drawback to wooden containers is that rot eventually sets in; they don't last as long as containers made from other materials. Some people sidestep this problem by setting pots inside their wooden containers.

The classic oak half-barrels and some teak containers will last for long periods without preservatives. Because of the ready availability of oak half-barrels, they are great containers for confining invasive plants like mint, artemisias, and lemon balm over many seasons, but more on that later as well. In general, however, oak and teak are quite expensive, although the half-barrels are usually available at a reasonable price. Pine, the most common wood for containers because of its low price, is also the quickest to rot. Several nontoxic wood preservatives may be used to greatly extend the life of wooden containers; check with your hardware store or garden center for a good selection. Avoid creosote and other preservatives that are toxic to plants.

Once considered past its prime, this old wooden box newly overflows with licorice plants, geraniums, and perilla.

Tea tins serve as temporary housing for seedling herbs. They're kept on the east-facing windowsill; hotter sun can roast the young roots.

Plastic containers have some uses—for instance, growing bog plants that have adapted to growing in oxygen-poor soil. Take special care when using black plastic containers that you do not end up making small solar cookers that will parboil the plants they contain. Plants kept in black plastic pots can often be tucked in the back of a grouping of plants to hide the container while shading it from the direct sun.

Metal containers also suit many herb-gardening uses. Metal containers can be made of steel, iron, brass, lead, or copper, and many are found objects. Steel containers may range from tea tins and milk cans to window boxes made specifically for plants. A coating of rustproof paint will help to extend the life of steel containers, and any metal container used for planting should have drainage holes.

Cast-iron pots and urns were once rather scarce but have again become fashionable and widely available. Cast-iron containers are extremely durable although they are heavy and difficult to move; nowadays the traditionally shaped urns are reproduced in lightweight aluminum.

Antique cast-iron urns were often painted to prevent rust, and new containers may be painted to achieve the same look.

Because unpainted containers may leave rust stains, situate them where this won't be a problem or seal them with paint or a clear plastic sealant before they are used.

Antique lead planters, which often began life as cisterns to hold rainwater, are almost prohibitively expensive. Reproductions, generally of lightweight fiberglass, are sometimes found at specialty shops.

Fiberglass containers, available in a variety of sizes and shapes, generally mimic the shapes and sizes of their lead, stone, terracotta, or wooden counterparts. Lightweight and durable, these containers are usually designed to withstand freezing temperatures, making them ideal for year-round use. Many, however, are quite expensive and may turn out to be a costly alternative to replacing less expensive containers occasionally. Like plastic and metal containers, fiberglass pots don't breathe and can heat up in direct sun.

Wire and plastic are frequently used to fashion hanging baskets. Plastic is lightweight, inexpensive, and holds moisture well but often looks more than slightly unattractive unless completely overgrown with plants. Wire containers make much more attractive hanging baskets, but in climates with low humidity, they dry out very

As the prices of antique urns have skyrocketed, other materials have been used to duplicate their appearance—at a reasonable cost. These cast-stone urns hold thyme, signet marigolds, and pansies.

quickly unless lined with a plastic container camouflaged with moss. Plastic liners for wire hanging baskets are available commercially or can be made from a piece of heavy plastic sheeting, but be sure to make at least three or four 1-inch-long slits in the liner for drainage.

Stone may be shaped to make some of most beautiful and most expensive containers of all. Limestone, marble, and sandstone are the three most frequently used materials for stone containers because they are the easiest durable stone to work.

Containers made of granite or other extremely hard stone are generally so expensive as to qualify as *objets d'art* and are seldom actually used for anything as mundane as plants.

Stone and the less costly cast stone and concrete containers are durable and stay cool, even in the hottest days of summer. They make ideal containers for public areas where less heavy containers might "walk off." Be sure to choose the site carefully; once you put them in place and fill them with soil and plants, these containers are very heavy.

Thyme, dianthus, campanula, and other alpine plants colonize a stone through.

HYPERTUFA RECIPE

Making hypertufa planters is as much fun as making mud pies and lots more productive. These planters are economical, attractive, and tough as nails, even in regions with harsh winters. Like mud pies, hypertufa is warm-weather fun because the material must not be allowed to freeze until it is thoroughly dry.

Start small when making planters. Use a large mixing bowl, a six-pack cooler, or similar-sized object as a mold. Protect your working surface with a sheet of heavy plastic. Turn the mold upside down and cover it with plastic, too.

We mix our hypertufa in a wheelbarrow—it's easy to rinse out. A couple of quarts of portland cement is a good quantity to start with; later you will get a feel for how much hypertufa will cover a particular size and shape of mold. Pull on your rubber gloves and your dust mask and start mixing.

One part portland cement
Three parts peat moss
Two parts perlite
Handful of fiberglass Fibermesh or similar product
Concrete colorant to taste (optional)
Water

Mix dry ingredients well. Add just enough water to make a thick paste.

Pat the mix around the bottom of the mold and begin working up. For a mixing-bowl mold, it can be about 1/2 inch thick, but larger molds require proportionately thicker walls. Press the mixture firmly onto the mold; make sure no air holes remain.

When you get to the top of the mold (which will become the bottom of the pot), make some holes for drainage and set dowels in them. Every day, wiggle the dowels a little so they will be easy to remove when the hypertufa is dry. After 4 to 8 hours, use a wire brush or another tool to add surface texture to the form.

Cover the form loosely with plastic so that it dries slowly. For the first few days, spritz the surface with water for even drying. Small containers can take a week or so to dry; large ones take three weeks or longer.

If you can't find Fibermesh or a similar fiberglass product, you can construct a wire foundation for the planter, but the fiberglass is well worth searching out. It's especially important to include it for strengthening large pots.

A cat-litter tray served as the mold for this hypertufa trough, now surrounded by Scotch thistle, rose campion, and Greek spitting cucumber.

One stone substitute deserves special mention: hypertufa. Once the exclusive playthings of rock gardeners, hypertufa containers are becoming more popular for a wide variety of plants. The material originated to mimic the old English stone sinks that were used to provide choice little alpine plants with high-and-dry growing environments through damp English winters. The original sinks are now nearly impossible to find, and discarded porcelain or stainless steel sinks just don't have the same charm. Hypertufa to the rescue! This simple formula makes an ideal container for growing plants—roots may actually grow into the pot's walls.

Hypertufa containers are usually low, wide troughs. We made several of these many years ago, and they remain in fine shape. Many older troughs were made over a chicken-wire or hardware-cloth foundation, but we've found that these often chip, and sometimes large chunks fall off, exposing the wire.

The simple hypertufa mixture can be shaped or molded into a variety of sizes and shapes, including some very presentable imitations of stone sinks. Wooden molds or plastic-draped bowls may be used as well. The wooden molds generally consist of two parts, one slightly larger than the other. If you're handy with a miter box, you can make molds with sloping sides.

We opted for the simpler method of plastering the hypertufa over inverted mixing bowls and roasters covered with plastic sheeting. We ended up with a little more "character" to some of our troughs than we'd intended, but nothing we couldn't live with.

Troughs are generally 1 to 2 inches thick and at least 4 inches deep. Before the hypertufa is completely set, make drainage holes about 1/2 inch in diameter in the container bottom; in large, flat troughs, make several.

After unmolding but before the hypertufa is completely dry, a light touch-up with a wire brush will disguise any surface imperfections, and a quick once-over with a butane torch will fuse any straggling bits of fiberglass and create an interesting surface texture by melting some of the perlite grains on the surface. Not everyone keeps a butane torch in the potting shed, but it's worth borrowing one when making troughs. Although hypertufa containers will probably not last for centuries like the old stone sinks, they're a whole lot lighter and easier to move.

BEYOND PLANTS, POTS, AND SOIL

Anyone who cooks has probably heard this lament at least once: "I'd love to start cooking, but I don't have the right equipment." A good cook's usual response is, "Start cooking, and you'll get the equipment you need."

The same is true for container gardening. To start, all you really need is plants, pots, and soil. Almost anything else is superfluous. Once started, you'll begin acquiring the tools that make the job a little easier. By then, though, you will know a lot more about what you really need and what will work.

That said, some acquired wisdom can be passed along to beginning container growers and shared among experienced ones. First, anyone who gardens will have most of the basic equipment for container gardening.

When beginning container gardening, get a couple of good, big covered trash cans. We keep one near the garden hose, and when we bring home a new batch of clay pots, in they go. As soon as we're ready to plant, we remove the pots that have been soaking and throw in the next set—no waiting. Otherwise, we keep the cans covered for the safety of critters in the neighborhood.

We keep a second can for soil storage and mixing. The lid keeps the soil dry and sweet until we're ready to begin filling pots. A trash can is also a great place to wet down potting soil before filling the pots; purchased potting soil often pours out of the bag as dry as bug dust. Once planted, it is almost impossible to wet thoroughly. It must be thoroughly mixed with water but not made into mud.

On the other hand, some manufacturers sell soil that is heavy with water. Potting soil and all of the ingredients for making it are sold by volume and not by weight, so don't be taken in.

We also keep a large trowel handy for filling pots. A plastic container will do the job if nothing else is handy, but a large trowel makes short work of mixing and wetting potting soil. It's also useful when transplanting plants into the containers.

Invest in a good trowel. Don't fall for the pretty painted trowels sold in the supermarket, shopping malls, and, it seems, street corners, every spring. These lightweight little numbers, when grabbed to dig up something that is far beyond their capabilities, promptly bend in half. Before we discovered the value of a good trowel, we amassed a huge collection of bent ones in the potting shed. As with all other gardening tools, our best advice is to decide what you can afford and then buy the next grade up.

Our small border spade fills large pots quickly. If growing in containers is your only foray into gardening, this tool might seem extravagant, but if you do enough gardening to justify one, you'll appreciate it. We use ours like a giant trowel; it's far easier to wield than a full-sized shovel. If you can't quite bring yourself to buy one, try dropping a few hints around the holidays.

Good cutting tools are probably next on the container gardener's shopping list. These accessories range from basic, utilitarian utensils to extravagant ones. We use our fingernails, scissors, paring knives, pocketknives, and almost anything else that will cut to tackle all sorts of chores. If you're like us, by the time your herbs have grown big enough to harvest and use, your fingernails are completely gone. If you use your scissors and paring knives for their intended purposes,

WHAT KIND OF PRUNER?

Many people seem confused about what type of pruner to buy—the bypass type, or the anvil type? Bypass pruners have blades that move past each other, like scissors, although usually only one of the blades is sharpened. Anvil pruners have a blade that meets a flat piece of metal. Either type works well so long as the pruner cuts cleanly without crushing the plant stem.

We have both kinds of pruners and normally use the pair we can find first, although bypass pruners generally will cut larger stems than the anvil type. Specialty pruners for container gardening range from miniature bypass and scissors types to fancy Japanese bonsai tools. Ah, yes, more things for holiday wish lists.

you may not want to use them to hack at your plants, too.

So you really do need something to cut plants with; you need pruners. These tools, like trowels and spades, come in all grades. A pair of utility pruners (or secateurs if you're French, British, or Martha Stewart) can be found in almost any gardener's toolkit. These work just fine for container gardening.

Last but not least on the tool list are watering accessories. Anything that does not leak too badly can be used to get water to a plant in an emergency, and we've used some strange watering cans on hot days to save new transplants from death. For growing herbs outdoors, we rely on a good garden hose and a water breaker. We spent years using cheap garden hoses that lasted only a couple of years. When a friend gave us our first good garden hose, we quickly replaced all of our cheap hoses with good ones.

We do all of our watering on the patio with a water breaker—a hose-end attachment that breaks the heavy torrent of a garden hose into an extremely soft shower. There are several types available, but most use the same type of water breaker, an aluminum-encased plastic spray head about 2 inches in diameter with dozens of fine holes. Most commercial greenhouses use them because they work extremely well.

If you're like us, by the time your herbs have grown big enough to harvest and use, your fingernails are gone. You need pruners.

A good water breaker is essential to our getting all the containers watered in a hurry without damaging the plants. Although the garden hose is on full blast, the stream is gentle enough for all but the youngest seedlings. We attach our water breaker to the end of an aluminum wand to reach plants in the back of the container garden; it improves our aim and makes spot watering more precise.

We also use a host of watering cans for plants in the house during winter and for fertilizing plants on the patio during the summer. In a pinch, any handy container will do, but a can or pitcher used only for liquid fertilizer or root-stimulator solutions is a must to prevent contamination.

Plastic and galvanized cans work equally well. The newer impact-resistant plastic cans can withstand tremendous abuse without springing leaks. Galvanized watering cans, however, have a good, solid sense of

Licorice plant, Cuban oregano, curry plant, and flowering maples overhang our collection of watering cans.

permanence. We keep a pair of 1 1/2-gallon watering cans and a 1-gallon plastic one in the house all winter. Trips to the faucet quickly become tedious with smaller cans, and larger ones are unwieldy.

We use cans with long spouts for watering the many pots we winter over on the porch. Our large galvanized cans have brass roses that produce a fine spray for fertilizing pots on the patio. The smaller plastic can comes in handy for watering small pots in the house.

For the water-soluble fertilizers applied during the summer, we rely on a hose-end fertilizer attachment that meters out the fertilizer, saving the effort of measuring it for every can of water. Ours comes with its own water breaker; at least one brand comes with a perfectly adequate plastic breaker that fits a standard garden hose coupling.

THE DIRT ON DIRT

Dirt is dirt.
Right?
Wrong. Any gardener will tell you all about the woes of bad dirt. Too much clay. Too much sand. No drainage. Won't hold water.

The ideal garden soil, loam, is only about half solid matter; the other half is composed equally of water and air, both essential to healthy plants. Only about 20 percent of the solid matter is organic material; the rest is ground-up or decomposed rock particles ranging from sand (the largest particles that qualify as soil) through clay, the smallest; particles in between are called silt. Most soils have varying proportions of these components; only a few qualify as loam.

Container gardening offers the chance to grow any herb in its ideal soil. Even if your garden soil is absolutely wonderful, it seldom works as well for plants in containers as it does for plants in the ground.

A good potting mixture of organic and inorganic components achieves both good

The recipe for lush, overflowing containers like these? It's simple: great dirt.

drainage and water retention. A simple maxim applies: light is right. Soil mixes overfilled with organic matter may retain water, but they can easily become waterlogged and drown plants. Others may let water wash through, retaining too little to keep the plant healthy.

Many commercial potting mixes are available by the bag, and most large garden centers sell them in bulk. How do you choose the right potting soil? That's a good question—we've been disappointed more than once. Most commercial potting soils are mixtures of peat, sand, perlite, vermiculite, compost, and/or topsoil. But some potting soils that look like dark, rich, beautiful garden soil have been colored with carbon for cosmetic appeal; check the labels. Special mixes are available for seed starting, growing cactus and succulents, and for general planting. Some come with fertilizer included—but only enough to last a single gardening season.

Each component of potting soil has its place in the mix. Topsoil, usually garden loam, is the basis for most potting soils. While a beautiful loam soil is every gardener's dream, other components must be added to make a good soil for containers.

Perlite, quartz sand that has been heated to extreme temperatures and popped like popcorn, and vermiculite, weathered mica keep the soil structure open, admitting air and promoting good drainage. Many gardeners prefer to use vermiculite because it does not float to the soil surface like perlite does. Some gardeners add coarse sand to potting mixes, especially soilless mixtures, to improve drainage, and keep highly organic mixes crumbly. Either material is suitable for use in container gardening.

As in the garden, organic matter improves the texture of the soil mix and holds both moisture and nutrients. Any gardener who has ever used a water-soluble fertilizer knows that the essential plant nutrients, such as nitrogen, phosphorus, and potassium (the N, P, and K respectively of fertilizer labels), dissolve in water. In fact, they must be dissolved in water to be taken up by plant roots. Organic matter holds these nutrients in a form that the plants can use.

Peat, ground bark, and compost provide organic material. Of the three, we much prefer compost. Peat is so long-lasting that it offers plants few nutrients; in addition, in some areas this nonrenewable natural resource is being depleted. We also dislike amending soil with ground bark or wood because it breaks down slowly. Compost opens up the soil and retains moisture. Because it is partially decomposed, it releases nitrogen slowly into the soil. We could add supplemental nitrogen if using peat or wood as organic matter, but we find that sticking with our home-grown compost as a soil additive gets the job done without fuss.

If you plant many containers each year, the cost of potting soil will soon catch up with you. And what should you do with the spent soil at the end of each season without unintentionally creating raised beds throughout your garden?

The answer is simple: recycle. We've been recycling our potting soil for more than a decade in inconspicuously placed garbage cans and chicken-wire hoops. Most of the old plants end up in the compost heap, but the roots stay in the potting soil to decay over the winter. Colorado's cold, dry winters don't encourage decomposition as well as other parts of the country, where consistent moisture and warm spells prevail; some years, we're mostly recovering the used soil instead of finding it enriched by the old roots.

In spring, we sieve the old soil and enrich it with new bags of soil, compost, and manure. Whatever has failed to decompose thoroughly gets tossed onto the compost pile.

PLANTING: PRACTICAL AND PRETTY

There are a few practical considerations about growing plants in containers. Water them too much and they rot; water too little and they parch. We avoid plastic pots that don't breathe to prevent the former; we use big clay pots that hold plenty of soil to prevent the latter. Pots smaller than 10

The sharp geometry of these heavy cast-concrete containers contrasts with their decorative contents, which include perilla, marigolds, dusty miller, and Verbena rigida.

or 12 inches in diameter dry out too quickly to be of much use except for cacti, succulents, and a few drought-resistant herbs.

Should you crock your pots or use squares of old wire screen to prevent soil from washing out of the hole in the bottom? No, because covering the drainage hole, even partially, impedes drainage, which can be fatal to the plant. If a pot sits on the ground, in a saucer, or on a cement block, how much of the soil can escape? We've never noticed that by the middle of July half the soil in our pots has suddenly vanished through a hole the size of a nickel. Place nothing in the bottom of the pot.

A small handful of gravel in the bottom of the pot does nothing to improve drainage; in pots with drainage holes, it simply reduces the amount of soil available to the plant. Worse yet is the mistake of substituting gravel in the bottom of a container for drainage holes; this produces a stagnant puddle of water that quickly sours and starts to smell like a truck-stop latrine.

It's not difficult to find compatible plant partners for pots. Many herbs demonstrate remarkable adaptability; favorites such as lavender, bay, chives, and rosemary thrive across most of the continent. Group the sun lovers together and the shade lovers together, and that's pretty much it.

Among these groups are plants that do best with wet feet and those that like to dry out a bit between waterings. Many Mediterranean herbs, for example, dislike constant moisture. Sun-loving lavender, santolina, rosemary, thyme, and oregano share a resentment of overly moist soil. Suitable companions such as globe amaranth, most species of *Plectranthus*, Mexican fleabane (*Erigeron karvinskianus*), scented geraniums, and mealy-cup sage (*Salvia farinacea*) also perform well when the soil dries somewhat between waterings. Plants that require sharp drainage benefit from a scoopful of small gravel mixed into their potting soil before planting.

Herbs that originated in moist, humid climates, such as basil, ginger, and perilla, suffer when they don't receive a constant supply of moisture. They combine happily with sweet potato vines, cannas, flowering maples, dahlias, and marigolds. Growing them in larger containers with moisture-retentive soil keeps them stress-free.

We advocate using large containers because of the irrigation factor. Although we water diligently and sometimes daily during the furnace-blast days of midsummer, we sometimes take a few days off during slightly cooler weather. Our big pots that start at 12 or 14 inches in diameter and depth hold plenty of plants. We expect the roots to delve down into the pots for nutrients and moisture, so we really stuff them in at planting time. A 14-inch pot might easily hold a gallon-size plant, several quart-sized ones, and a few six-pack plugs. It could also hold up to five quart-sized plants and a few plugs, or a whole bunch of plugs.

There's no formula. If it fits, plant it. Don't leave lots of space between plants—jamming them in makes burgeoning, billowing containers. Because the growing season is relatively short and we want results quickly, not a week before frost, we plant the root balls tightly together and work extra potting soil into the cavities between them to keep the roots from drying out. It's important to firm the plants in well to get the roots in contact with the soil so they can anchor themselves.

Some people balk at squeezing plants together so tightly. Think of the containers as summer camp dormitories: though the quarters are cramped, it's for only a relatively short time. Like kids, the plants will survive just fine, especially if they're kept well fed.

Don't fill the pots up to the rim with soil and plants, however, because then you can't water the plants in thoroughly. That first thorough soaking is the most important.

Where frost rarely threatens and a container is a more or less permanent feature, plants may be initially planted with more space between them and periodically pruned and renovated. Feature specimens, such as topiaries or large lavender plants, benefit from a topdressing of fresh soil once or twice a year. Scrape out the top few inches of soil in the pot and replace it with fresh,

Tips for Planting

Some potting soil is too dry, so mix it with water until it is damp and well saturated. This may require overnight soaking. Drippy soil, however, may drown fine plant roots.

Roll the plants gently from their small pots and spread their roots out a little. If the plant is rootbound—the roots have filled the container—you may wish to straighten them and trim them back by about a third.

Roots need soil, so make sure it completely surrounds them. Allow no airholes around the plant roots or elsewhere in the soil.

Tamp the soil down lightly but firmly as you fill in around the roots.

Place the plants' rootballs tightly together for rapid fill-in.

Water the plants into their new pot. Gently and thoroughly soak the soil, checking to be sure that the container drains well.

Think of jam-packed containers as summer-camp dormitories for plants. These campers include Cuban oregano, fancy-leaf geraniums, golden marjoram, oxalis, and mint.

David's Assembly-Line Planting

Over the past several years, we've developed methods for getting all of our pots started in the spring.

The first step is staging most of the empty pots around the patio, leaving spaces for the plants that wintered over in the house. We use concrete blocks, bricks, benches, cracked pots, and wooden blocks to vary the height of our containers. After we've arranged the pots—and rearranged them at least once—we start mixing the potting soil.

I scoop the potting soil from our motley collection of containers that have held it over the winter, sieve it through a 1/4-inch mesh screen directly into a wheelbarrow, and add a generous amount of fresh, well-rotted compost. If the soil is very dry, I run some water into the wheelbarrow with a garden hose and stir with a small border spade. This part of the operation can turn into real work, so if I have time, I stretch it out over a few days or even a couple of weekends. When the soil is done, I truck it straight to the patio.

In the meantime, we've made innumerable trips to nurseries for flats and flats of plants for the containers. From the basement and porch, we've hauled all the seedlings, cuttings, and the plants held over the winter. All of these must rest for several days under the trees.

When the plants have hardened off, we switch into high gear. Color schemes have been determined for different areas of the patio, under the folly, and along the side of the house. Plants are stuck into pots as fast as we pull them out of their nursery containers. First we do the large plants for each pot, and at the second pass "tart up the pots" by stuffing every remaining bit of pot space with small plants. Most of the pots get one or two annuals, such as nasturtiums, helichrysums, or perilla, to give continuity to the plantings in each area.

Rob finishes tarting up the pots, and I begin hauling water to the newly planted containers. New pots always get a weak dose of fertilizer for their first drink; it gives them a good jumpstart.

The container garden is never complete. We frequently rearrange pots to show them off to their best advantage or to hide their flaws. Most trips to the nursery or even the big discount stores involve new plants for both the garden and the patio. Few people are interested in container gardening on this scale, but we've seldom had anyone visit the garden who didn't enjoy the results. I certainly doubt that anyone has more fun at it than we do.

nutritious soil—it only takes a few minutes. Pot-bound herbs should be transplanted to pots just a size or two larger. Eventually a plant may get so big that you can't move it to a bigger pot without a crane. Then top-dress and feed it regularly in its cramped quarters—and consider bonsai training for its replacement.

WATERING: THE HOSE GAME

Photographs in glossy magazines show containers gardens stuffed to the max with beautiful plants. The plants tumble gracefully from their handsome clay pots and speak of luxurious abundance. It all looks so lush, lovely, and almost effortless. Almost.

We're equally guilty of showing off the best plantings, not those that somehow went awry, but we will gladly tell you that behind every great pot is a gardener—with a hose. Those exquisite photographs don't show the work that goes into creating a pretty, productive grouping of containers. Once it's all put together, each grouping needs periodic grooming, fertilizing, and—especially—watering. Sometimes help comes from the skies, but at some point, most of us face a period of high temperatures and low rainfall—and the daily chore of watering. Whether a gardener tends a single, lonely pot of basil or 600 pots of assorted plants as we do, watering is inescapable in midsummer.

Some of our friends rely on high-tech drip systems for their containers. These free the gardener from the task of watering, but they must be cleverly designed and masked from view. They must also be dismantled and stored during winter except in frost-free climates. This all seems like too much hassle for us, and it doesn't account for adding new pots or rearranging at whim.

We'd just as soon spend some daily quality time with our plants. Plants with high moisture requirements get a good long drink whereas we skip over the drought-resistant ones. Compost and other organic matter help to retain moisture in some pots while plants that like wet feet sit in saucers, and those subject to rot have their pots elevated by decorative feet.

It takes about half an hour to complete the watering, but it's not a waste of time. It gives us a chance to take a look at each

Whether a gardener tends a single, lonely pot of basil or 600 pots of assorted plants as we do, watering is inescapable in midsummer.

plant to see how it's doing, perhaps stick a finger in the soil to see if it needs water at that moment. If aphids or whiteflies have moved in, we're more likely to spot them early and battle them with a soap spray before they get out of hand. There are moments, too, when we simply pause to admire and appreciate the sights and scents of the container garden. Some might consider watering to be a tiresome, boring chore. Not us.

Experience is your best guide to watering plants. Lift smaller pots to check for moisture—especially indoor plants. Water is heavy, and a light pot is ready for a good soaking. Probably the most common cause of dead container plants has less to do with Mother Nature than with Mother Hen. Overly solicitous gardeners tend to water their container plants to death. We've stressed the importance of proper drainage for containers and potting soil, but almost any plant can still be drowned.

The first symptoms of overwatering look very much like those of underwatering. The plant begins to droop and looks dry. Soon it turns yellow, then brown, and begins to drop leaves. Inexperienced gardeners may pour on more water to compensate, but the problem is that the roots are rotting and cannot take up water—despite the water, it is dying of drought.

If you suspect that you're killing a plant with kindness, dump it out of its container and take a look at the roots. Healthy plants have a large number of new, fine, white roots. The roots of overwatered plants are nearly all brown. If there's hope for the plant, cutting back on water will help it revive. Be patient, though, because it will take a few days or weeks to recover and begin to put out new growth. It may lose even more of its leaves before it adjusts.

When watering is sometimes done on the run and a plant appears to be getting too much water, taking the saucer out from under it sometimes solves the problem. If that doesn't do the trick, set the pot up on bricks or pot feet to improve the drainage and take special care to reduce watering. Many of our cacti, succulents, and other dryland plants get a 1/2-inch mulch of pea gravel, a visual warning not to linger too long with the garden hose. The mulch also helps prevent rot by keeping the plants from coming in contact with damp soil.

Summers with monsoon moisture may make it easier on the gardener (and the water bill), but it's very difficult to keep pots from becoming waterlogged—pot feet go from decorative to indispensable, and all clay saucers ought to be removed until dry weather prevails. If heavy rains continue for more than a few weeks, your life is miserable anyway and losing a few potted plants may be at the bottom of your list of priorities. It's still worth it to drag them to a dry

Drought-tolerant succulants share a patio with thirstier herbs; outstanding foliage contrasts create drama.

porch or shed or set up a makeshift rain barrier.

Hail often accompanies summer squalls. We get hit periodically, and it's always dazing and depressing, as if Mother Nature had punched us in the stomach. We drink heavily for a few days after a hailstorm, and then we prune heavily and compost the damaged leaves. Hail damage wounds leaves, inviting infection, so we often must prune once-handsome plants down to mere stubs. Hail usually pulverizes annuals like basil, perilla, and summer savory to mush, a total loss, but many perennials and tropical plants may regenerate from the roots if stimulated by a little added nitrogen in their regular fertilizer.

If underwatering seems to be the problem, first try adding a saucer beneath the pot. Another way to saturate overly dry soil is to water the plant in the sink, perhaps allowing water to flow through the pot several times, and letting it drain thoroughly. You can also place plants on a tray of wet gravel to raise humidity around the plant. This little trick is useful indoors during the winter, when the air in many homes feels like the Sahara.

On extremely hot days, plants may wilt. Don't mistake this for a sign of underwatering. If the plants perk up as the temperatures begin to drop, the heat of the day has caused them to temporarily shut down. Although plants use large amounts of water during summer heat, be sure to check the soil for moistness before grabbing for the garden hose.

Fast Food: Fertilizer

All plants require sunlight, water, and air. They also need nitrogen, phosphorus, and potassium in relative abundance and several others in lesser amounts. Given all the light, water, and air that a plant requires, these are the limiting nutrients for growth.

When a plant is growing in the ground, nitrogen is provided from several sources. Although the gas is abundant in our atmosphere, plants can't use it in that form. In nature, lightning "fixes" nitrogen by combining it with oxygen and hydrogen to form compounds that dissolve in water. Certain bacteria in the soil fix nitrogen on the roots of legumes, and decomposing animal manure releases nitrogen as well.

Phosphorus and potassium are present in fairly large amounts in the minerals that make up rocks. Like nitrogen, they must be dissolved in water before plants can use them.

As dead plants decay, all these nutrients are released as water-soluble compounds; removing dead plants prevents these nutrients from returning to the soil. Water also washes nutrients away from the plants' root zone, so they must be replaced, particularly for plants in pots, for continued performance. Even the best potting soil loses nutrients before the end of the growing season as water passes through it.

We're not true organic gardeners. We try to be as environmentally friendly as possible, but we use chemical fertilizers. Once nutrients are in a form that its roots can take up, a plant can't distinguish where they originated.

There are several ways to fertilize plants. Using dry fertilizer, while convenient, can be akin to playing with fire—literally. Too much dry fertilizer can prevent the plant roots from taking up water and "burn" the plant. Coated fertilizer pellets release nutrients slowly over a long period of time, eliminating burning. Our main objection to coated fertilizer, however, is that you generally have to make do with one type of fertilizer throughout the growing season. We like to be a little more proactive in our plant feeding.

We use water-soluble fertilizers throughout most of the growing season, but we change fertilizers as the plants' needs change. In the spring, we feed containers about every week with a high-nitrogen fertilizer (perhaps 20-20-20) because nitrogen promotes new green growth. (Lawn fertilizer is almost all nitrogen to give turf that golf-course look.)

Lots of leafy container herbs, such as basil, parsley, and kale, can get by with a 20-20-20 mix throughout the growing season. For plants that bloom, however, we cut back on the nitrogen after the early feedings and use a 10-20-20 mix to boost flower production.

To go organic, amend the potting soil with bone meal for slow-release phosphorus, lime (definitely not for most of the alkaline West), and a small amount of nitrogen. Liquid kelp is a good source of minerals. Add about a quarter cup of each of these ingredients to 20 to 30 gallons of potting mix.

A llowing the old plant roots to decompose over the winter and enriching the soil with fresh material each year will provide adequate nutrients for most herbs.

With a little common care, potting soil can be recycled for years. Just remember that all the nutrients your herbs will use must come from the soil in the pot plus anything extra that you add. Allowing the old plant roots to decompose over the winter and enriching the soil with fresh material each year will provide adequate nutrients for most herbs. Then work a handful of balanced organic fertilizer into each pot in the spring or add liberal doses of water-soluble fertilizer throughout the growing season.

FROM HERE TO INFIRMITY: PESKY BUGS

Mother Nature is not always kind to gardeners, and container gardeners don't get any kind of break. Containers offer a chance to control many of the variables that affect plants, but lots of things can happen.

Container plants are prey to aphids, mealybugs, scale, whiteflies, and powdery mildew. Occasionally leafhoppers, thrips, caterpillars, earwigs, slugs, black vine weevils, black spot, rust, virus, gray mold (*Botrytis* spp.), and damping-off attack container plants. Like most other gardeners, we've had bouts with these problems. Sometimes we've even solved them before the plant dies—but not always.

Most pest and diseases are opportunistic: they attack weak or stressed plants. Heat stress, water stress, and situating plants in either too much or too little light makes them easy victims.

The key to keeping plants healthy is to avoid plant stress. Proper watering and regular fertilizing keeps stress to a minimum. If you notice diseased plants among your collection, discard them immediately—don't even think about composting the plants or recycling the potting soil. Toss it all out. Plant diseases carried by recycled soil may infect a new generation of plants, and even the prolonged cold of a hard winter does little to stop some plant pathogens.

Insects often transport diseases from plant to plant, especially sucking insects like aphids and thrips, so keeping plant pests under control helps keep plants healthy. We've discovered, as much through negligence as through study, that the least aggressive approach to pest problems is often the most effective.

Using insecticides as a last resort supports a healthy garden ecology that includes predator insects. We count ladybugs, lacewings, predator wasps, spiders, and birds among our best friends in controlling pests and diseases in the garden.

Although pests and diseases may be unavoidable, identifying the problem is the first step to finding a cure.

Aphids. Aphids are a colorful breed of pest: they may appear in black, green, or red, but they seldom add anything to the aesthetics of a container planting. These are little creatures, generally less than 1/4 inch long, that usually appear in groups on new growth and buds, sucking away at the plant's sap. During some phases of the life cycle, aphids sprout wings to move from plant to plant. They multiply at an enormous rate: a newborn aphid (and most are born rather than hatched) may reproduce within a week or two. Most don't waste time mating—they're born pregnant. Some aphid species lay eggs late in the season to overwinter; others survive as immature or adult females.

Aphids often excrete plant juice as a clear, sugary liquid called honeydew. This attracts other insects, including wasps, bees, flies, and ants. Ants are so fond of honeydew that they often "farm" aphids on plants and can be seen moving aphids on the plant and harvesting the honeydew from them. The sweet sap may cover the leaves of the infested plant and is sometimes noticeable on other surfaces.

The honeydew is a perfect growing medium for black sooty mold, which in some cases covers entire leaf surfaces and prevents photosynthesis, starving the plant.

A severe infestation of aphids may kill a plant or at least distort the growth tips. Aphids also spread viruses from plant to plant, which is often a more serious problem than their sucking.

Luckily for us, aphids are rather clumsy creatures with fat bodies not built for speed. Ladybugs, and especially ladybug larvae, find them easy prey. An adult ladybug eats from ten to twenty aphids a day, and a larva devours between twenty and thirty. Lacewings and other predators also help control aphids. Almost any insecticide will control aphids, but by reducing the numbers of predators, it may make the problem worse in the long run.

Another way to get rid of aphids is to dislodge them with a blast of cold water. They seldom return to reinfest the plant. A bath with soapy water will also do them in.

Scale. Scale insects often infect container plants, primarily woody ones. Unlike

Spider mites have damaged this plant; they love hot, dry conditions and natural predators rarely control them.

most insects, they spend most of their lives under protective shells and don't move. They look like bumps up to 1/4 inch in diameter on plant stems or the undersides of leaves. Like aphids, scales suck plant juices; the plants they attack eventually look water stressed.

Of the two primary types of scales, armored scales can kill even large trees, but soft scales seldom proves lethal. Soft scales, like aphids, can produce large amounts of honeydew.

Scales most frequently attack plants under stress. Keeping plants watered and fertilized is the best defense.

Ladybugs and parasitic wasps are the best natural controls for scales. Oil spray or insecticidal soaps smother them without significantly reducing natural predators. Scales can be scrubbed away using fingernails or a toothbrush, but heavily infected shoots and leaves should be pruned and discarded.

Spider mites. These leggy little pests can cause extremely large problems. Spider mites are usually detected by the damage they do, the first sign often being spots on plant leaves.

Spider mites are very small—less than 1/20 inch long—and they usually live on the undersides of leaves. More closely related to spiders than insects, they are eight-legged arthropods that may be brown, red, green, or cream. When infestations are heavy, they may build a very fine network of webs on the undersides of the leaves. The insects are best spotted when they are moving or by checking with a magnifying glass.

Spider mites are most active in hot, dry weather and can move from plant to plant on the wind. The natural enemies of spider mites, such as black ladybugs, lacewing larvae, and predatory mites, seldom prevent mites from reaching damaging numbers.

As with most other pests, the best prevention for spider mites is healthy plants. A strong spray of cold water will help dislodge the mites, but sulfur dust or insecticidal soaps are more effective. Several conventional pesticides can be used to control severe infestations, but be sure that the label specifically includes "mites" and the name of the plant you are trying to treat, and follow the label instructions.

Mealybugs. These disgusting pests are tiny, aphid-like creatures covered by waxy filaments of gray, white, or pink. Slow-moving and soft-bodied, these pests usually hang out on plant stems and where leaves join the stems. Insecticidal soaps or light oil sprays control mealybugs or, if you have the patience, they can be removed by a cotton swab dipped in alcohol.

Leafhoppers. Leafhoppers also make their home on the undersides of leaves, but they're a bit easier to spot because they hop when the plant is disturbed. These sucking insects, less than 1/4 inch long, can be controlled with insecticidal soaps. Use a soaking spray, however, to be sure to score a direct hit. Several conventional insecticides, including pyrethrum, rotenone, and Sevin, will offer more reliable control but should be used only in cases of severe infestation.

Thrips. Tiny thrips, less than 1/8 inch long, drive gardeners to distraction. Thrips infestation generally shows up as a silvery discoloration of leaves and white spots on flowers. A friend who works for a large commercial greenhouse near Denver has nightmares about thrips infestations. Insecticidal soaps can be effective, but thrips, like leafhoppers, generally require thorough soaking with a fine spray to control them. Greenhouse operators frequently resort to extreme measures to control thrips because they resist many conventional insecticides.

Whiteflies. Here's another minuscule pest that can cause major headaches. When airborne, the brilliant white adult whiteflies can be seen hovering around plants; the immature ones look like flakes or scales on the undersides of leaves. They multiply so rapidly that only a few quickly produce hundreds and thousands. We've learned the hard way to eradicate whiteflies as soon as we spot them. We've had infestations that looked almost like dust storms when the plants were disturbed.

We control whiteflies by washing the plants frequently with insecticidal soap.

Major infestations may require three or four washings at three- to four-day intervals. We've also had good luck with pyrethrum-based insecticidal sprays. Yellow sticky traps also help reduce their numbers.

Where the temperature falls below freezing, whiteflies must survive indoors. It's always a good idea to check for whiteflies when buying plants, but even stock from the best greenhouses and nurseries can harbor a few of these little pests.

Slugs and snails. Slugs and snails seem to enjoy fresh herbs and greens as much as people do. While Denver's dry climate discourages these slimy little creatures in some situations, in well-mulched gardens or greenhouses here and elsewhere they find plenty of suitable habitat.

Slugs and snails—especially slugs—seem almost endemic to greenhouses. Even urban rooftop gardeners living in high-rises find damage from slugs brought in with new plants. In the overall scheme of things, slugs make themselves useful by recycling dead plants and returning nutrients to the soil. Alas, they also have a taste for green leaves, especially young, tender shoots.

The first signs of slug damage are irregularly shaped holes in leaves or at leaf margins. Careful inspection will often show silvery trails of slime left by the crawling slugs or snails. Several brands of slug and snail bait are commercially available; they're effective against pests in ornamental plant-

David's War with Whiteflies

Our first encounter with whiteflies came when we began raising tomatoes. The tomatoes were planted in the sunniest spot in our small vegetable garden, next to a brick wall to hold as much heat as possible. The tomato cages were overflowing with vines, and it looked as if nothing could go wrong. In fact, we had already harvested a few tomatoes for luscious bacon, lettuce, and tomato sandwiches.

Then the vines began to fade, and the leaves lost some of their glossy shine. It had never occurred to us that the plants' problems might have something to do with the tiny white insects we saw looping lazily around the vines.

One day I looked at the underside of a tomato leaf and found it covered with tiny white insects and dozens of tiny, clear eggs. So that's what was killing my tomato plants!

I headed to the shed and read the labels on every insecticide in my arsenal and filled the sprayer with something lethal. But just a few days later, I found myself spraying the whiteflies again. During my third whitefly foray, I yelled to Rob that the only whiteflies I was killing were the ones that drowned.

Enough was enough, I thought. If I had to drown them, I'd do it right. This time around, I filled the sprayer with water and a liberal dose of liquid castile oil soap and thoroughly enjoyed washing down the tomato plants. I repeated the process a few days later, but by then the whitefly population had taken a nosedive. After a couple more doses, the problem was under control and I didn't have to worry about being poisoned by eating the sprayed tomatoes.

One beautiful fall day a few years later, while drinking my morning coffee on the back porch and staring off into the sunny garden, I noticed that the air was full of floating spider webs. I realized that the only chemical we'd used on the garden regularly was liquid soap. The garden was filled with spiders, ladybugs, lacewings, and all sorts of other predators feeding on other creatures. There hadn't been any need to use anything more toxic. When problems crop up in the garden now, I grab the liquid soap first.

Where you find moisture-loving plants, slugs and snails may well be lurking nearby. Our partially shaded patio features golden sweet-potato vine, scented geraniums, flowering tobacco, and abutillon.

HERBS IN POTS

ings, but not to be used on edible plants.

Container gardens raise the plants above ground level so that they are inconvenient for slugs and snails. These pests feed at night and seek damp, dark hiding places during the day. At the first signs of slug damage, check under the pots during the day to find the culprits, then mash them.

Less violent but equally benign control methods include slug traps loaded with nontoxic baits. These traps typically lure slugs into containers where they become trapped or drown. We can't testify to the effectiveness of homemade traps, but some make sense. We've tried a jar lid filled with beer; the slugs like the beer but drown in it. The drawback is daily cleaning of the traps and disposal of their gross contents.

Another is to turn empty grapefruit or cantaloupe halves upside down near plants that slugs have damaged. In theory, the slugs hide in the fruit shells, only to be tossed out before their next foray into your plants. And yet another: wet a section of the newspaper, roll it up, and secure it with rubber bands. The slugs that hide in the tube can be tossed easily into the trash. We're not sure just how effective the last couple of traps are, but they're cheap and easy to try.

Some gardeners report excellent control of slugs and snails—there's no such thing as total elimination—by encircling pots with copper collars. Cut thin sheet copper from the craft or hardware store in strips 2 or 3 inches wide and as long as necessary to encircle the pot's rim. Fold the strip in half lengthwise, then cut halfway through the width every inch or so. When the strip is bent into a circle, the effect is like a spiked dog collar, with sharp edges to cut the tender underbelly of a slug or snail if it dares to try to cross it. Nail the strips onto wooden containers. To attach them to a terra-cotta pot, poke holes near the ends of the strip, lace wire through, and tighten by twisting with pliers so that the collar won't slip down. We've been told that the copper carries a slight electric current that also repels most of the critters from the barricade. These copper rings are not unattractive and develop the classic weathered patina in time, making them less obtrusive.

Gardeners with too much time on their hands and a sturdy pair of metal shears could come up with some decorative scalloped patterns, like embroidery on pillow shams. This sounds like a winter project for the half-crazed, housebound gardener.

POT PATINA: PARSLEY, SAGE, ROSEMARY, AND SLIME

Do we paint our pots with buttermilk to encourage the formation of moss? Get real. Who has time for that?

It seems peculiar that some aficionados want a sterile, freshly scrubbed pot to put plants in, while others demand slimy, moss-encrusted ones. We once saw a celebrity gardener on television advising people to spray their pots with shellac or water seal so that the pots would stay new looking. Following this silly suggestion would nullify any benefit to using a clay pot, since it would stop the pot walls from breathing, depriving the roots of oxygen, which is vital to good root health.

Plants in clay pots thrive when they get the amount of light, water, and nutrients they need. We don't worry about fertilizer salts that build up on the walls. They've leached out—they can't return to the soil to hurt the roots, although these salts may signal that your plants are getting too much fertilizer.

Moss doesn't seem to do a bit of harm, either. At the moment, it's considered highly picturesque. Our pots never grow much moss, mainly because we live in a semiarid climate with low humidity.

An easy way to achieve that mossy look is to thin a moss-green, water-based paint with water and paint it on the pots. Such pots look suitably aged, decrepit, and expensive.

But we don't have time for this either. It seems like a lot of fuss over pots that within a month or so of planting have almost completely disappeared underneath their inhabitants. By the middle of summer, our bleachers of pots against the house are almost hidden beneath the sprawling and cascading vegetation. More than one visitor has commented on the "beds" next to the house. We like that—it means that our motley crew of potted plants has become more than the sum of its parts—it's a true garden.

The Winter of Our Discontent: Off-Season Storage

After the first hard frost has taken its toll, we spend a few minutes regretting the end of the season and then get back to work. It's tempting to ignore the mess and retreat into the house for the winter, but the clay pots must be emptied and stored, even if the wind is raw and our resolve is low.

An empty dry clay pot, turned upside down and protected from moisture, will make it through the winter in good shape. On the other hand, a pot left upright and filled with soil may be ruined. Its walls stay damp, and the alternate cycles of freezing and thawing can crack or flake the clay. Good terra-cotta pots are too expensive to treat so rudely.

We store our empty pots beneath benches, under the eaves of the house where it stays dry, or under the roof of our folly. Some gardeners cart their pots to a storage shed or garage (cars always get the short end of the stick in a gardener's house) or spread a sheet of plastic over them.

No terra-cotta pot lasts forever, but even the simplest winter protection will help to prevent damage. Winter seems to drag on endlessly, but when it comes time to pot up again, it's good to have a dry collection of pots at our disposal.

We bring many tender herbs into our home, but it's no picnic for them. Our old house is drafty and cold, and they don't exactly flourish. Most survive, however, and that's fine.

Some perennial herbs stay outdoors to fend for themselves, and we're often amazed by what survives. Depending on the severity of the winter, we find fresh sprouts in late March on potted thyme, chives, lungwort, ivy, creeping celery, motherwort, artemisias such as 'Valerie Finnis' and 'Powis Castle', santolina, salad burnet, and sage.

We don't recommend leaving these potted herbs outdoors during a Zone 5 winter because plants, like pots, are vulnerable not only to cold but also the deadly effects of alternating freezing and thawing. To improve the plants' survival rate, we cluster the pots of these hardy plants on the north side of a massive juniper that blocks the sun and traps snow. The north side of a fence or building (especially near a foundation) offers the same sort of protection. Cold frames, storage sheds and other outbuildings, unheated garages, and unheated porches offer a bit more protection. We heap them with mulches of straw, leaves, or boughs to moderate the extremes of winter.

This wooden tub, full of leafy lettuce and surrounded by sweet alyssum and catmint, wears a copper collar to ward off slugs and snails.

The overall idea for these overwintered potted perennials is to keep them evenly cold, not warm. Damage and death results more often from the roller-coaster ride of up-and-down temperatures than from cold.

The roots are more vulnerable in a pot than they would be in the ground, so normally stalwart perennials don't always come through. Still, it's worth the chance, since we don't have room inside and most perennials need a winter chill, or so it seems to us. An autumn-dug trench is a great idea—snug and cozy, especially when pine boughs or straw cover the pots inserted into it—but we never think of that until the middle of winter.

Wherever they are sheltered, potted herbs need water. They don't need much when it's cold and snowy, but during an open winter, we lug a few cans of water to them. We wait to prune and cut back until spring is well under way. Early pruning encourages young growth that succumbs easily to freezes, weakening plants that have already had a tough time. We think they deserve a break.

CHAPTER 2
THE COOK'S PATIO

WHEN ASKED WHY HE BEGAN cooking as a hobby, a friend declared, "Everyone needs a hobby and everyone has to eat." Cooking has changed tremendously in the past few years. A decade ago, if a favorite recipe required herbs, you either used dried herbs, waited until summer, or sought them out in specialty stores. Now the selection of fresh herbs in supermarkets is astounding, even if we've begun to take it for granted.

Although it's handy to pick up fresh chives, basil, cilantro, dill, and other herbs at the store, it's even nicer to have them on hand at the back door or on the windowsill. Americans have become concerned with more than just the taste of food and want a healthy diet with reduced salt and fat, too. We're not obsessive about food, but few things improve the quality of home cooking more than fresh ingredients, especially fresh herbs.

It's easy to fall back on old, familiar habits in the kitchen. We both grew up in homes where salt and pepper were often the only seasonings for an entire meal, and a peek into many spice cabinets will reveal dust-coated boxes and tins of herbs and spices at the back of the top shelf. Yet anyone can pick up a good cookbook and find new herbs being used in interesting ways.

Fresh herbs quickly broaden the palate. Many, such as chives, basil, and cilantro, retain little of their fresh flavor when dried. These and many other herbs are easily grown year-round on the patio or a sunny windowsill.

Basil (*Ocimum basilicum*). A staple in Italian cooking, this versatile herb can flavor far more than spaghetti sauce. It's wonderful on fresh tomatoes, eggs, fish dishes, or in almost any other savory

A bonanza of perilla backs up the bright leaves of nutmeg-scented geranium and coleus.

recipe. Some basils have spicy or lemony flavors.

Basil is easy to grow from seeds started every couple of months to keep a fresh supply on hand. All basils like warm weather and bright sunshine; they're one of the few plants that thrive when transplanted into patio containers in the hottest weather. They require a moderate amount of water and do not take kindly to drying out. Basil foliage varies from the fine leaves and rounded forms of 'Spicy Globe' to the huge green leaves of lettuce-leaf basil to the dark burgundy of 'Red Rubin'.

Basil normally sets seed in the fall, or earlier in some climates, and dies, so keep plants growing as long as possible by pinching off the flower heads. You may find perennial or East Indian basil (*O. gratissimum*) at your garden center or listed in a seed catalog. The flavor is similar to that of annual basil, but we advise that you try it before you grow it as your only basil plant—you may find it does not suit your palate.

If you grow an overabundance of fresh basil, freeze it in water or olive oil; it retains little flavor when dried. For sauces and stews, we chop the basil leaves, put them in ice cube trays, and fill the cells with water. We repackage the frozen cubes in plastic freezer bags. It's easy to drop a couple of basil cubes, straight out of the freezer, into a pot of simmering soup or stew.

We also freeze small quantities of basil in olive oil for making pesto—basil mixed with pine nuts, garlic, olive oil, and parmesan cheese—that is practically indistinguishable from that made with fresh basil. Pesto makes a great spread on crusty French bread or a tasty topping for pasta, especially when combined with crumbled bacon or thin slices of spicy Italian sausage.

Bay laurel (*Laurus nobilis*). This is one of the first herbs we began growing in a container. The price of a small jar of bay leaves in the supermarket will pay for a small bay tree. In all but the warmest climates, the tree must be brought indoors for the winter, where it is a model houseplant when placed in a sunny window. Bay does not require much water, especially during the winter, although we killed our first one by letting it dry out too much. But we salvaged its dry leaves by using them in cooking.

Bay leaves are potent. They're often used in pickling mixes and are essential in bouquets garnis, small packets of varied seasonings used to flavor stocks, soups, and stews. A leaf, or even half a leaf, is enough to flavor a quart of stew.

Borage (*Borago officinalis*). The cucumberlike flavor of borage's dainty blue blossoms delicately enhances sauces for fish and aspic, and they have been used to decorate fruit or wine punches and tisanes since the time of the ancient Romans. The plant may grow to 2 feet tall and sprawls; it requires a very large pot. An annual, borage is easily grown from seed in a sunny location and may self-seed under favorable conditions. Borage flowers are best used fresh; when dried, they have almost as much flavor as wheat straw.

Salad burnet (*Sanguisorba minor*). Tender, finely toothed leaflets of salad burnet, often the first greens to appear in spring, are unfamiliar to many Americans, but Italians add them often to salads. Some describe their flavor as similar to cucumber but definitely more complex. More mature leaves taste bitter, so only leaves from the plant's center are harvested.

This perennial herb thrives in full sun or partial shade with moderate moisture, reaching a height of up to 30 inches. Salad burnet's dainty foliage, reddish stems, and pink flower heads contrast well with the larger maroon leaves of red basil or chard.

Chamomile, German (*Chamaemelum nobile*). The small daisylike flowers of German chamomile are harvested worldwide for a relaxing tea, but they also make a fine addition to beef stock. This plant's annual cousin, Roman chamomile (*C. recutia*), looks similar but has a hollow, conical center of the flower compared to the German chamomile's solid flower center.

The fine-textured, creeping plant adapts nicely to dish gardens; it also serves as a trailing plant in pots or hanging baskets of mixed herbs. The foliage smells delightfully

Handsome lettuces adapt to container plantings along with cool-season herbs such as chervil.

of apple. The most attractive form of chamomile is the double-flowered 'Flore Pleno'.

Chervil (*Anthriscus cerefolium*). Chervil, sometimes called French parsley, joins parsley, tarragon, and chives to form the traditional French *fines herbes*. Its slightly anise flavor is tasty in fresh salads and delicately flavored savory dishes. Vinaigrettes, especially those destined for fruit salads, benefit from its inclusion as well. Chervil is a required ingredient in authentic béarnaise sauce, a delicate mixture made primarily of egg, butter, and wine.

A finely textured annual herb, chervil's lacy, light green leaves take on a pinkish blush during the summer. Its clusters of tiny white flowers appear in late summer, and the plant goes to seed quickly in hot weather.

Chervil grows best in pots with moist soil, protected from the afternoon sun. Seeds should be started every few weeks to ensure an ongoing fresh supply of tops. Dried chervil lacks flavor, and even the freeze-dried herb pales in comparison to fresh.

Cilantro (*Coriandrum sativum*). Coriander and cilantro come from the same plant: coriander is the seed, and cilantro is the leaf. We both grew up enjoying the taste of coriander seeds, which flavor the center of jawbreaker candies and are used in dishes ranging from apple pie to pickles. Mature seeds are aromatic and have mildly spicy flavor, but unless you are growing lots of this herb, the seeds are too few to harvest.

Cilantro is reputed to be the most widely used herb on earth; certainly it's essential in southwestern, Chinese, Caribbean, and Indian cooking, just for starters. For many Americans, however, cilantro is an acquired taste that some compare to a particularly aromatic parsley. Use it fresh; like so many other herbs, cilantro's flavor flees upon drying or, despite the best attempts of salsa makers, canning.

Cilantro leaves resemble those of Italian parsley, but they're a lighter green. This cool-weather herb quickly sets seed when the temperature climbs too high, so plant seeds at frequent intervals to keep the fresh herb on hand; slow-bolting varieties are now available.

To use this herb, pick the leaves any time. Harvest seeds, if you wish, just as they turn brown but before they drop. Spread in a shallow pan to dry a few more days; pick over carefully. For the best flavor, store the dried seeds whole for up to several months before using.

Dill (*Anethum graveolens*). Nearly every American recognizes the flavor of dill from tasting dill pickles. Now the herb shows up in everything from dips for vegetables to flavored potato chips. Although freeze-dried dill is a reasonably acceptable substitute for the fresh herb and dill seeds retain

Kale's huge, lacy rosette is accented by nasturtiums, Italian parsley, and other herbs.

THE COOK'S PATIO

65

their characteristic flavor for years, neither quite matches the taste of fresh dill. Nothing complements the flavor of fresh grilled salmon like a few sprigs of fresh dill.

Dill's threadlike foliage can be added fresh to salads, sauces, and dressings. It also combines well with other pungent herbs such as chives, garlic, and onion. The seed heads can be harvested like those of coriander.

Fennel (*Foeniculum vulgare*). Many people who visit our garden know about fennel seed and how to use it in Italian dishes, but the tall, feathery plant itself is a surprise. We're always giving visitors a pinch of the leaves to taste the pleasant, aniselike flavor. We like fennel in salads—either as a green or a flavoring in salad dressing. Because we rarely dig mature plants from our borders, we seldom eat the roots. In the past few years, however, we've noticed that they are turning up as a raw or lightly cooked vegetable in many recipe books.

We grow fennel almost everywhere—the bronze-leaved variety makes such an attractive foliage plant that it's hard to resist. It also self-sows vigorously, so resis-

We like fennel in salads—either as a green or a flavoring in salad dressing, but we seldom eat the roots.

tance is futile. We let it reach its full height—up to 5 feet tall—in borders, but in pots fennel's finely textured foliage makes it a great filler. We treat the young plants as annuals.

Fenugreek (*Trigonella foenum-graecum*). Long used in India as a spice for curry and chutney, fenugreek remains uncommon in American kitchens. In Middle Eastern, Indian, and African cooking, the seeds are an important ingredient; they taste somewhat like celery.

The herb, an annual, reaches a height of 1 to 2 feet, with foliage resembling that of clover. The seeds require about four months to mature, so in cooler climates, like Denver's, plants must be started indoors several weeks before the frost-free date. Fenugreek loves sun and heat, so in areas where a four-month growing season is assured, start the plants outdoors after the danger of frost is past.

Fenugreek's small, intensely fragrant white flowers are followed by pealike seedpods up to 6 inches long. When the pods turn brown, uproot the plant and hang it upside down to dry in a warm, shady place before removing the seeds from the pods.

Geraniums, scented (*Pelargonium* spp.). We're constantly running across new, enchanting varieties of scented geraniums that bear fragrances of rose, ginger, apple, oak, mint, lemon, lime, tangerine, coconut, strawberry, nutmeg—everything except garlic or bubble gum, and those may be out there somewhere.

Many people use the leaves of scented geraniums in potpourris or to scent linen cabinets, but few use them in cooking. They may never become staples, but the leaves of those with rose, peppermint, or apple scents can be used to flavor sweet baked goods, custards, and cooked fruit.

In the container garden, scented geraniums are almost foolproof. They thrive on heat and sun and don't mind small containers that allow them to dry out between waterings. Their plant and leaf forms and textures are nearly as variable as their scents. We grow the gamut from rigid, upright, small-leaved lemon-scented varieties through the large, fuzzy-leaved, trailing mint ones.

All scented geraniums die if frosted, so we bri   freeze and,   ignore them   ey get weekly waterings but usually lose most of their leaves. As the days get longer in the spring, we try to increase the amount of water and cut back leggy growth. We root the cuttings under lights in the basement

A stroll past this grouping of scented geraniums is a sensory delight.

and set them out when the danger of frost is past. We give them water and fertilizer at regular intervals.

Despite this unceremonious treatment, within a few weeks of being set outdoors, the scented geraniums look as though they are fresh from a greenhouse. What could be easier? With plenty of light and a little more attention, they can be kept presentable all winter.

Horehound (*Marrubium vulgare*). We thought horehound candy tasted horrible when we were kids, but *M. vulgare* is a beautiful plant both in the garden and in containers. Although the spikes of small white or lavender flowers can reach 2 feet tall, the plant may be kept trimmed to a more manageable size. Horehound does best in full sun and doesn't need much fertilizer. As with many other perennial herbs, pots of horehound can be wintered over in a cold garage, cold frame, or cool porch. The soft, fuzzy leaves make a beautiful foliage complement to any container grouping.

Hyssop (*Hyssopus officinalis*). Named for an ancient herb to which it is probably unrelated, hyssop is itself an ancient herb that was popular for strewing during the Middle Ages. It has also been used for seasoning game and to add a mildly bitter flavor to salads and fruit.

Hyssop is an ancient herb that was popular for strewing during the Middle Ages. It also serves to flavor game, salads, and fruit.

Hyssop plants grow 2 to 4 feet tall and bloom throughout the summer in blue, pink, or white. This perennial can be started from seed in the spring or fall or bought as nursery stock. Hyssop is hardy in Zones 3 to 9 when planted in the ground; potted hyssop may be wintered over indoors or allowed to go dormant in an unheated garage or porch.

Lavender (*Lavandula* spp.). Judging by the number of cultivars available, lavender is a plant breeder's delight. Plant encyclopedias may dedicate several pages to the basics of lavenders.

We grow *L. angustifolia* because it's one of the few species that is hardy in our Denver garden. Tender *L. stoechas* and *L. dentata*, however, make great container plants for the patio. Lavenders thrive in hot, sunny locations similar to their Mediterranean homeland.

Most of us think of lavender as an herb for sachets and linen drawers, but the

Fresh thyme straight from the garden is likely to impart more complex and elegant flavor than dried.

flowers also hold a useful, if somewhat limited place in the kitchen cabinet. The flavor goes well with any roasted meat, especially turkey and pork. David uses lavender flowers (sparingly) as part of a seasoning mixture when cooking turkey. He sprinkles the dried blossoms, along with thyme, savory, sage, rosemary, and whatever else strikes his fancy on a butter-saturated cheesecloth that protects the turkey from becoming too brown during roasting. Frequent basting of the cheesecloth with the pan drippings gives the turkey and gravy a wonderful, subtle flavor.

Lemon balm (*Melissa officinalis*). We made the mistake of introducing lemon balm in our old garden, where it quickly got out of hand. Now we keep it confined to a pot but still watch it warily. Its crinkled green leaves make an appealing lemon-scented garnish for iced teas, fruit salads, and gazpacho. The gold-leaved form is

We think strawberry pots are worthless for strawberries, but pretty darn good for sage, scented geraniums, and rosemary.

even more attractive. As you might guess, this herb grows easily in any pot in sun or partial shade.

Lemongrass (*Cymbopogon citratus*). Lemongrass, a staple throughout much of Southeast Asia, is a tender perennial grass that provides a graceful linear element in container plantings. We bring lemongrass into the house during the winter and keep it under low-light conditions. By spring it looks almost dead, but the leaves it loses over winter are nearly as flavorful as the fresh ones.

Lemon verbena (*Aloysia triphylla*) (syn. *Lippia citriodora*). Lemon verbena is a tender shrub that must be grown in containers anywhere winter temperatures fall below 40°F (4°C). Although not a particularly spectacular plant, its lemon fragrance more than recommends it. A South American native, lemon verbena is either easy to grow or easy to kill; the general consensus seems to be that it grows best in a container at least 12 inches in diameter in well drained, slightly alkaline soil and full sun in all but the most southern latitudes. Organic matter in the soil seems to help if counterbalanced by a little lime. Lemon verbena tolerates too little water better than too much. The plant can get a little leggy, so it benefits from an annual trim. If you can keep lemon verbena alive, you can end up with a 5-foot-tall shrub in a decade or so.

Marjoram and **oregano** (*Origanum* spp.). *Origanum* is one cool genus. There are so many wonderful oreganos, not all of them cooking herbs. A friend at the Denver Botanical Gardens once went through a love affair with the genus and scouted out some of its stranger species; many are worth growing just for fun.

The most important marjorams for the kitchen garden are sweet marjoram (*O. majorana*), wild marjoram (*O. vulgare*), and pot marjoram (*O. onites*). The first is a tender perennial and the other two are hardy perennials, but all can be grown in containers. Several other plants have been called oregano; one is Cuban oregano (*Plectranthus coleioides*), which does not belong to the genus. Wild marjoram and pot marjoram grow to about 2 feet tall, and both "open up" when their pretty lavender-pink flowers open, changing

A South American native, lemon verbena is either easy to grow or easy to kill; the general consensus is that it grows best in a container.

abruptly from a bushy, upright plant to a floppy, spreading mess. New growth then begins in the center of the plant, and the outside stems can be cut and dried.

Sweet marjoram grows about a foot tall and looks great spilling down from a pot or hanging basket. Although fairly tolerant of a range of soil, it prefers a dryish, alkaline environment. It winters over easily in a sunny window.

Mints (*Mentha* spp.). If there ever were plants that ought to be grown only in container gardens, mints are at the top of the list. Spearmint (*M. spicata*), peppermint (*M. ×piperita*), and, to a lesser degree, apple mint (*M. ×villosa* var. *alopecuroides*) quickly become thugs if turned loose in the garden. These perennials spread by underground runners and will easily choke out any other plants in the vicinity. Mints can be confined only by large stretches of concrete or asphalt or periodic applications of napalm.

All of the mints, including the smaller and noninvasive Corsican mint (*M. requienii*), have attractive foliage and small, pale purple or white flowers. They're good foliage plants in container groupings, but they're best when relegated to their own containers—the larger the better. Because they spread so rapidly, they perform best if repotted annually. During the winter, mint pots can be stored in a cool garage or porch or sunk into a cold frame. It's possible to keep mints in the house over winter, but they need very bright light; cut back straggly plants periodically to promote fresh leaves.

Pot marigold (*Calendula officinalis*). Pot marigolds are sometimes called poor man's saffron, and some grocery stores sell their dried petals for coloring food. The beautiful yellow color that pot marigold imparts to cooked food resembles that of true saffron (*Crocus sativus*), but pot marigold does not have the same flavor or intense color.

Pot marigolds can be used in containers in the same way as garden marigolds (*Tagetes* spp.), with the added bonus of tangy edible flowers. The foliage of pot marigolds more closely resembles that of hybrid zinnias than that of garden marigolds. The stress of summer's high heat invites aphids while slowing their growth and flowering, so we usually pull out and compost the pot marigolds in midsummer.

Nasturtiums (*Tropaeolum majus*). Growing up, Rob thought nasturtiums originated on another planet. The stems are offset from the center of the round leaves, which taste peppery like watercress. The flowers make a colorful and tasty addition to salads or an edible garnish.

Nasturtiums are easily started from the pea-sized seeds. They sprout best if soaked in water overnight before planting. There are both bushy and trailing varieties of nasturtium, but we're especially fond of using the trailing varieties to spill from the rims of containers. We're quite taken by the variegated 'Alaska' and use it to enliven both pots and plates.

Parsley (*Petroselinum crispum*). A biennial herb, parsley must be grown from seed every year. There are three different types of parsley: curly (*P. crispum* var. *crispum*), plain or Italian (*P. crispum* var. *neapolitanum*), and turnip-rooted (*P. crispum* var. *tuberosum*). Each variety includes several cultivars, all easily started from seed. Both curly and plain parsley are widely available as plants in the spring and throughout most of the summer.

In European cuisine, parsley is a staple. Although available in any supermarket, the herb grows cheerfully in a pot year-round. Parsley resents drying out completely and requires full sun to grow and maintain a healthy green color. It can be included in annual container plantings on a sunny deck or patio or can be grown on a sunny kitchen windowsill. If you don't have enough sunlight indoors to grow parsley or other herb that require bright light, use a fluorescent light to supplement the sun.

Perilla (*Perilla frutescens*). Sometimes known as Chinese basil or shiso, perilla is an annual with metallic red leaves about the size and shape of basil leaves. Although we don't do much Asian cooking and have to admit that we've only nibbled the herb, it's unusual to find a container without perilla

Perilla and peppery nasturtiums look terrific against a background of burgundy fountain grass.

in our garden. Perilla seeds seem to have saturated every cubic foot of potting soil on the place, and we're happy as clams. The seeds sprout as soon as the weather warms up. The plants go to seed after the truly hot weather sets in. By then, though, the rest of the plants in the containers have filled in and the perilla has fulfilled its role as an early filler.

Perilla is available in two green varieties, one with plain leaves and one with curly leaves, and both plain and curly-leaved varieties in red. We call the curly-leaved red perilla "deVil," after Cruella; the metallic sheen of the dark maroon leaves is almost surreal—like something made out of plastic flecked with gold paint. Compared to the others, it sets seed later in the season.

Chives (*Allium schoenoprasum*). We use chives both in the kitchen and on the patio with nearly equal fervor. Chive blooms are a pretty mauve, and their grasslike foliage adds a strong linear element to a container without adding stiffness.

David uses chives in the kitchen to substitute for scallions, to provide a mild onion flavor, or to use when the last of the green onions have turned to slime in the bottom of the vegetable bin. Chives are easily grown from seed—as any gardener knows who's let them seed in the garden. They're also easily transplanted, either from nursery-grown stock or from an extra self-sown clump from the garden. Because chives are so easy to grow, they're a must for winter windowsill gardening.

*T*o fresh summer tomatoes, we add a bit of fresh basil, chives, freshly ground, black pepper, and balsamic vinegar to make a great salad.

It's hard to resist eating the first few ripe garden tomatoes completely unadorned, but when the novelty has worn off, we add a bit of fresh basil, chives, freshly ground black pepper, and balsamic vinegar to make a great summer salad.

To keep potted chives looking good, harvest them by cutting a few of the tubular leaves near the base of the plant instead of bobbing the top. Chives cut to the ground grow back vigorously, but we don't like the flat-top look on the patio. If you want to keep your plant around for the long run, be careful not to overuse it. Like other members of the onion family, chives require the foliage to keep the bulbs alive. Continuous trimming of a single plant eventually weakens the bulb and results in spindly foliage. If you're addicted to chives, you may want to keep more than one pot around to let one recover while using the other.

Garlic chives (*Allium tuberosum*). Garlic chives, first cousin to common chives, have an endearing white flower. The leaves are flat and coarser than those of common chives and carry a mild garlic flavor. In late summer, the starry, sweet-scented white flowers add floral sparks to containers.

Peppers (*Capsicum* spp.). Peppers run the gamut from sweet pimentos and bell peppers to fiery jalapenos and serranos. What constitutes a "hot" pepper varies from region to region: serve peppers that are considered mild in Texas to Mid-westerners, and you might be accused of attempted murder.

All peppers have one thing in common: they love heat—hot weather, that is. And all of them, from hot Thai or ornamental pepper topiaries to big bushy pimento plants, resent cold weather. In Colorado, our spring nighttime temperatures often dip below 50°F (10°C), a magic number for young peppers. Below this temperature, the plants will stunt and may never recover.

Some plant breeders offer varieties that claim to be cold tolerant, but these have limits. Our trick to getting peppers off to a good start is planting them in containers that can be snuggled up to the brick walls of the house. Although we live in chili country and dried and roasted chili peppers are available everywhere in the late fall, David has a strong penchant for pimentos. Their bold glossy foliage looks great in a pot, and the bright red fruit is beautiful in late summer.

Rosemary (*Rosmarinus officinalis*). We envy Californians their beautiful rosemary shrubs and can't help brushing our hands across them as they tumble over retaining walls just to release the clean, piney fragrance. The herb of friendship, loyalty, and remembrance, rosemary is widely available either as small starts or elaborate topiaries.

Keeping rosemary through the winter is not always easy. The herb requires lots of light, and the soil should be allowed to dry out between waterings—but beware of overwatering afterwards. We hate to admit it, but not all of our rosemary plants live through the winter; the ones that don't end up in the cooking pot or potpourri bowl.

Savory (*Satureja* spp.). Savory hasn't earned the notoriety of many of its mint-family cousins, and it offers a flavor reminiscent of thyme and marjoram (some say with hints of lavender) and an easy-growing nature, making it a natural for container gardening. Summer savory (*S. hortensis*) and winter savory (*S. montana*) are the most common; a third, *S. douglasii*, is sometimes called yerba buena, although other herbs are sometimes identified by that common name also.

All of the savories do best in light, well-drained soil, and yerba buena needs relatively dry summer conditions to thrive. These creeping plants trail over the edges of containers in full sun. Savory flowers are attractive to bees, but trimming summer savory's flowers keeps it from setting seed and going the way of all annuals.

Sorrel (*Rumex* spp.). Sorrel has been used as an herb since Greek and Roman times. English or garden sorrel (*R. acetosa*) and French sorrel (*R. scutatus*) are both commonly grown, but French sorrel has the best flavor for cooking in soups or eating raw in salad. The two varieties are similar in form but may be distinguished by the shape of the leaves: English sorrel has long, spear-shaped leaves and French sorrel has smaller, more heart-shaped leaves. Because oxalic acid gives sorrel its distinctive flavor,

David's favorite cooking herbs—thyme, basil, chives, and sage—share a pot just a few feet from the kitchen door.

it shouldn't form a major part of anyone's diet. We still can't resist a few leaves in spring salad, and the young leaves (which also have the best flavor) contain less acid than the older ones.

Because sorrel heralds spring with its early growth, we grow it in a half-barrel where it can spend the winter outdoors. It grows best in full sun. To keep the plant looking fresh, remove the flower stalks as soon as they appear. On the other hand, the dried flower stalks, with their reddish clusters of flat seeds, may be used in dried arrangements. It's your choice.

Sweet cicely (*Myrrhis odorata*). Sweet cicely, with its long, tenacious taproot, is another good candidate for growing in a half-barrel or other large frost-proof container. Sweet cicely prefers a semi-shady setting and produces a finely cut foliage similar to chervil, which gives rise to its other common names, sweet chervil and giant chervil. The seeds take up to eight months to germinate, and after several years the plant may reach a height of up to 5 feet, so growing sweet cicely requires a certain amount of commitment.

The leaves, seeds, and roots of sweet cicely have a mild anise flavor and can be used to replace part of the sugar in tart fruit dishes. The leaves can be added to salads, and the roots, like fennel, can be cooked or eaten raw. The clusters of small, white flowers make a pretty, edible garnish.

Tarragon, French (*Artemisia dracunculus* var. *sativa*). This anise-flavored perennial is the only tarragon worth growing for cooking. Russian tarragon (*A. dracunculus*) may look similar to French tarragon, but its flavor is nearly nonexistent. Because it does not set viable seed, French tarragon must be propagated by cuttings or division.

Most of us have a jar of dried tarragon in our spice cabinet, although the herb loses most of its complex flavor during drying. Keeping sprigs of tarragon in vinegar is a much better way to preserve the subtlety of the fresh herb. Use pickled tarragon leaves just as you would fresh ones, in fish, egg, cheese, chicken, and meat dishes.

You may either grow potted tarragon as an annual or keep it in containers that can be left outside over the winter, such as oak half-barrels. Tarragon's soft green foliage makes an excellent background plant in groupings of containers. Avoid overwatering and overfertilizing, or the plants may become floppy; a light midsummer feeding is enough to keep the plant growing from year to year. Dividing the plants every three of four years keeps them vigorous.

Thyme (*Thymus* spp.). Thyme is one of the most versatile herbs in the kitchen, garden, or container. There are literally hundreds of species and cultivars of thyme, from relatively large-leaved mother-of-thyme (*T. pulegioides*) and tiny-leaved *T. minus* to the the small, shrublike culinary thyme (*T. vulgaris*). Thyme is rarely used as a major flavoring agent; instead, it beefs up the flavor of other herbs. Lemon thyme (*T. ×citriodorus*) and caraway thyme (*T. herba-barona*) offer interesting variations on the basic flavor.

Because of their stature, most forms of this perennial herb make excellent candidates for trough gardens. Thyme thrives with periods of winter dormancy but resents winter dampness, making troughs the ideal solution. Troughs made of hyper-tufa resist winter freezing and thawing and show off any form of thyme to advantage. When planted in a container, the rapidly growing mother-of-thyme will quickly cascade over the rim.

Culinary Pots: Variations on a Theme

Herbs have done amazing things for our diets. Neither of us grew up with adventuresome cuisine; we knew only the staples of Midwestern cooking. Americanized versions of Italian or Chinese cuisine occasionally made their way into our white-bread enclaves, but we had no idea that the world was filled with wonderful culinary delights.

Growing herbs has brought fabulous surprises to our kitchen. We can't cover every ethnic cuisine that we experiment with and enjoy, but we'd like to explore the wild world of culinary theme pots. They're designed to group commonly used herbs for several popular schools of cooking—for instance, Italian, Mexican, and Oriental. The herbs for any particular style of cooking—Greek, Indian, Moroccan—can be concentrated in a single pot with a diameter of at least 18 to 20 inches or in a grouping of several containers. Some herbs are widely used in many cultures, while some are exclusive to one country or region. You don't need an enormous garden with rows and rows of vegetables and herbs to enjoy an ethnic dish made with fresh herbs.

One of the keys to enjoying the fresh herbs from the container garden is flexibility. Most good cooks who garden have learned to take a look in the garden before planning a meal. Is there an abundance of fresh basil? A good loaf of French bread with fresh pesto might be a good way to start tonight's dinner. Substitutions and additions of different herbs can keep your cooking fresh and spontaneous.

Pesto, for example, need not be limited to fresh basil; a wide variety of herbs, including parsley, thyme, oregano, savory, or rosemary, may be added to fresh basil or even substituted for it. A simple plate of sliced tomatoes can be a spectacular side dish with the addition of a little olive oil, balsamic vinegar, and whichever fresh herbs are at their peak—basil, chervil, oregano, parsley, rosemary, chives, or savory. We're not trying to write a cookbook, but we hope that you'll try out some of our ideas and, better yet, come up with some grand inventions of your own.

EVERYBODY SALSA

Mexican food is hot. Cooks across the nation have discovered the south-of-the-border taste sensations of tacos, tamales, burritos, and chimichangas. Many gardening cooks find acceptable spices, seasonings, and produce at their local supermarkets, while other cooks prefer to grow their own ingredients. They may cultivate the variety of pepper most compatible with their own taste buds, all the way from warm to five-alarm. The onions they grow may also be tailored to their own palate or even their sense of color. And the tomatoes—well, there's no substitute for a juicy, home-grown tomato, even if there are innumerable cultivars from which to choose. Some people can't stand cilantro; we can't do without it, but we sometimes substitute flat-leaved Italian parsley if we have guests who don't share our enthusiasm.

Put these ingredients altogether and they spell salsa. Store-bought brands may serve well enough in winter, but no self-respecting Mexican chef puts up with salsa from New York City or anywhere else when fresh ingredients are on hand. The pleasures of fresh salsa (or gazpacho, picante sauce, pico de gallo, or whatever concoction you prefer) enliven summer evening meals and add fire to dinners when the bite of frost grips the autumn garden.

The potting mix for a salsa pot should be fertile and well drained. Regular watering and fertilization ensure good yields. Tomatoes and peppers don't need a lot of nitrogen; in fact, both produce an excess of

COOLING THOSE CHILI PEPPERS

If you can't stand the fire of hot peppers but still want the flavor, remove their seeds and white membranes, the parts that hold most of the heat in the form of capsaicin. Wear rubber gloves when handling hot peppers—the capsaicin is very difficult to get off your hands, even with soap and hot water.

If the peppers are still too hot for your palate, try chopping and then soaking them for an hour in a cup of water with about 2 teaspoons of salt or vinegar added. If this doesn't work, try a milder variety.

How to Roast a Pepper

To roast one or two peppers, skewer them on a wooden-handled fork and turn them over high heat or an open flame until the thin skin begins to crack and blister. Place in a towel or plastic or paper bag until cool, then scrape the skin off with the tip of a sharp knife and discard.

To roast a number of chili peppers, put on your rubber gloves and cut the peppers open. Remove the seeds and membranes and flatten the peppers. Place skin side up on a cookie sheet and broil until the skins are blistering and in some places burned black. Slide the peppers off onto a kitchen towel and wrap tightly; wrap the bundle with plastic wrap. When cool, open the bundle and scrape the skins off the peppers.

leaves at the expense of fruits if they receive too much. Tomato varieties bred for compact growth may prove more manageable in pots than large, bushy kinds. Some kinds are especially intended for patio containers and hanging baskets. These compact hybrids usually need no staking and often mature earlier than other types.

Tomatillos, also called Mexican ground cherries or husk tomatoes, adapt easily to life in containers and can be grown just like regular tomatoes. Although canned tomatillos are widely available, we like the fresh ones better. We don't use large quantities, so growing them in containers is an ideal way to maintain a small but steady supply in late summer. One tomatillo is enough to add a distinctive, slightly sour taste to a large batch of salsa.

Basil, chives, chervil, Italian parsley, marjoram, and thyme are all easy additions to the salsa pot and can come in handy for more than just Mexican cooking. Iced tea is the perfect beverage to accompany a fiery Mexican meal; grow some sweet Aztec herb (*Phyla scaberrima*) to flavor it.

Onions and garlic may also be grown in a salsa pot. Where space is at a premium, consider buying these ingredients because the taste of homegrown onions and garlic doesn't vary much from store-bought produce. When space is ample, grow your own. We like the option of growing our favorite kinds of onions and harvesting some early as green scallions.

Almost any type of chili pepper can be grown in containers, from sweet bell peppers to hot jalapenos, but they must be protected against temperatures below 50°F. Serrano, banana, Fresno, rocotillo, and jalapeno peppers are commonly used in salsa.

Gazpacho, anyone? Add a bush-type cucumber plant to your salsa pot for most of the basic ingredients for gazpacho, the classic chilled Spanish soup. Gazpacho is essentially a salsa made from bell peppers, tomatoes, cucumbers, and onions. Chives, parsley, basil, chervil, oregano, and a cautious amount of hot peppers enliven this refreshing, nonfattening lunch, which is a good thing after all the sour cream and cheese we used to top those burritos, flautas, and quesadillas.

Our salsa is usually the outcome of Rob's protesting that it's too hot while David sneaks in just a few more hot peppers. However it turns out, we like salsa on just about everything. We attack a fresh batch with tortilla chips or ladle it over a cool summer salad of lettuce, avocado, and cold

BASIC FRESH SALSA
Makes about 1 cup

This classic garnish can be used to fire up tacos, grilled meat, poultry, eggs, and fish. The "heat" of the salsa varies not only with the number of chilis added, but the type as well. Banana peppers, for instance, are chilly chilis compared to jalapenos.

2 large tomatoes, peeled and chopped
1 medium onion, peeled and chopped
1 clove garlic, crushed
2 or more chopped serrano, banana, Fresno, or rocotillo chilis, fresh or roasted, seeds and membranes removed, finely chopped
2 tablespoons or more chopped fresh cilantro, or 3 sprigs Italian parsley, chopped
1 teaspoon salt
1 teaspoon chopped fresh marjoram, or a dash of dried marjoram (optional)
Dash of ground cloves (optional)

Mix the chopped vegetables and seasonings. A green or red jalapeno may be added for a hotter salsa. For variety, add a little chopped basil, fresh oregano, epazote, or fresh thyme, as well as fresh lemon or lime juice to taste.

Basic Gazpacho
Makes about 6 cups

Try this cool, low-calorie soup at the end of a hot summer day.

2 large cucumbers, peeled and seeded
3 large tomatoes, peeled and seeded
1 large bell pepper, seeds and membrane removed
1 Spanish onion, chopped
1 clove garlic, peeled and finely chopped
3 cups beef, chicken, or vegetable broth, or water
Juice of 1/2 lemon or lime, or 1/4 cup apple cider vinegar
1 tablespoon olive oil
1/2 teaspoon paprika
1/4 cup chopped chives
Salt to taste

In a blender, puree one-third of the vegetables with enough liquid to make a smooth liquid. Add to remaining vegetables and liquids, chopped chives, and paprika. Salt to taste. For a smooth soup, puree all of the vegetables.

For variety, you may substitute parsley, basil, chervil, tarragon, or a blend for all or part of the chives. Try substituting a small finely chopped green or red chili, seeds and membrane removed, for the paprika. Serve chilled.

Pico de Gallo
Makes about 1 cup

This fiery condiment, best prepared by hand, is not for the faint of heart.

1 large tomato, peeled and seeded
4 fresh jalapeno peppers, seeds and membranes removed
1 small onion, peeled
2 tablespoons or more chopped cilantro
2 tablespoons vinegar or lemon or lime juice
Salt to taste

Finely chop the tomatoes, peppers, and onion. Add the remaining ingredients and mix well.

chicken. And, of course, we smother every hot Mexican dish in salsa.

Because David likes his Mexican food inordinately hot, he also uses the hottest of peppers for a special batch of his favorite condiment, pico de gallo. It's amazing how much sweat can pour from one man's brow—we set his place with a napkin and a headband.

THAT'S ITALIAN

There's no such thing as "Italian cooking," but many people envision lasagna, spaghetti, and all sorts of pasta at the mere mention of these words. Who doesn't salivate at the thought of a classic Italian dish made from fresh garlic, tomatoes, oregano, thyme, mushrooms, cheeses, and all those other yummy ingredients?

A pot or grouping of pots for this style of cooking could easily include Italian plum tomatoes (a favorite at our house), eggplant, thyme, oregano, garlic, onions, Italian parsley, and marjoram, with different plants for Mediterranean cuisines ranging from southern France and Spain to Greece and Turkey.

BASIC PESTO
Makes about 1 1/2 cups

Count the number of cooks who love pesto, and you'll find at least that many variations of the basic combination of herbs, nuts, cheese, and olive oil.

2 packed cups fresh basil leaves, washed and dried
2 cloves garlic
1/2 cup pine nuts
1/2 cup freshly grated parmesan cheese
3/4 cup olive oil
Freshly grated black pepper, to taste

Chop basil and garlic to a coarse paste in blender or food processor. Add nuts and cheese, and process briefly. Add olive oil in a thin, steady stream while continuing to process.

Variations: Substitute pecan for the pine nuts, or use lemon basil with almonds. Try cilantro with toasted pumpkin seeds, oregano with walnuts, or mint with cashews.

Tomatillos, tomatoes, jalapeno peppers, Aztec sweet herb, and cilantro fill this pot with flavor.

HERBS IN POTS

Let the tomato or eggplant serve as a centerpiece with the thymes and oreganos as fillers and spillers. Depending on the size of the pot or the space for the grouping, feel free to add other herbs and flowers of the southern Mediterranean region such as dianthus, santolina, and rosemary. These aromatic herbs add to the beauty of the grouping, and their fragrances are sure to inspire the creativity of the chef. All are easy to cultivate in well-drained soil on a sun-drenched patio or windowsill.

TEA TIME

For the summer tea season, we keep mints and other tea flavorings in pots near the kitchen door. Who wants to sprint out to the garden on a hot day for a sprig of mint or blade of lemongrass? If we didn't keep them nearby, we wouldn't use them.

All varieties of mints—peppermint, spearmint, chocolate, apple, and lavender, to mention only a few—work wonders on a pedestrian pitcher of iced tea. We usually add them along with the ice, but a leafy stem dropped in with the tea leaves before pouring in the hot water gives the tea more zing. The boiling water turns it limp and brown, of course, so a few fresh leaves can top off the glass when it's served.

Some tea lovers grow hanging baskets stuffed with a variety of favorite mints. Others confine them to a large container, such as a half-barrel, to fight it out among themselves. Most mints can overwinter outdoors in Zone 5 or warmer areas.

In tea, we prefer the herbal tastes of lemon balm, lemon verbena, and lemongrass to the taste of lemon itself.

We grow other tea herbs for variety. Lemon balm, lemon verbena, and lemongrass impart lovely but differing hints of lemon flavor to a glass of chilled tea. A little sugar, honey, or Aztec sweet herb emphasizes the lemon flavor. We prefer these herbal lemon flavors to the taste of lemon itself. Scented geranium leaves from the citrus group may be added during brewing to create other subtle tastes. Rose-scented geraniums also work well. We wouldn't recommend the geraniums with odd scents like oak-leaf or nutmeg, but then we've never tried them.

Tea drinkers who prefer a brew without caffeine—or without true tea (*Camellia sinensis*) altogether—may want to grow pots of chamomile and red clover for their flowers and fennel, angelica, lemon balm, hyssop, and thyme for their fresh leaves.

Cloves or cinnamon are other favorite additions to our teas, but we go to the cabinet rather than to the patio for them. As a general rule, use one teaspoon of dried herbs, or two teaspoons fresh, to each cup of freshly boiled water for tea.

Basil meshes beautifully with pineapple sage and Verbena patagonica.

These containers leave little doubt as to the use of their inhabitants: tea herbs Roman chamomile, various mints, and scented geraniums.

POSTHOLIDAY TURKEY CASSEROLE
Serves 4 to 6

This isn't exactly a stew, but we love it and use the same herbs as in a more typical stew.

3 medium potatoes, peeled and cut into 1/2-inch chunks
1 medium onion, chopped
2 medium carrots, sliced 1/4 inch thick
1 large rib celery, sliced
2 cups chicken or turkey stock
3 tablespoons chopped parsley
1/4 teaspoon fresh thyme leaves
1/2 teaspoon paprika
1 bay leaf
Slivered fresh or crumbled dried sage to taste (optional)
1 cup turkey gravy, or 3 tablespoons flour shaken in 1 cup milk
1 cup cooked vegetables such as green beans, peas, corn, or broccoli
1 teaspoon salt
1/2 teaspoon freshly ground black pepper
1 1/2 cups cooked turkey, cut into 1/2-inch chunks
Dough for Buttermilk Biscuits (follows)

Preheat the oven to 425°F.

In a large saucepan, boil the potatoes, onion, carrots, celery, and herbs and spices in the stock until the vegetables are tender. Add the gravy (or flour and milk) along with the cooked vegetables and return the mixture to a boil; if the mixture is too thin, add more flour and milk. Stir in the salt and pepper and fold in the turkey. Pour into a large, flat, ovenproof dish. Top with the biscuits and bake for 15 minutes or until the tops of the biscuits are nicely browned.

Years ago, a single bay leaf was thought a daring addition to a hearty beef stew, but no longer. A creative cook today might consider planting any number of delicious herbs for use in savory dishes, including stews and casseroles.

The whole *Allium* tribe, from chives and onions to garlic, shallots, leeks, and garlic chives, are indispensable. Leafy herbs such as basil, celery, chervil, costmary, fennel, fenugreek, parsley, sage, savory, tarragon, marjoram, oregano, and thyme all are likely to become part of a cook's repertoire when the real thing is available.

Take care, however, if you aren't familiar with using fresh herbs. Begin with twice the amount of fresh herb as dried, as dried herbs are more concentrated. Experiment

BUTTERMILK BISCUITS
Makes 8 to 12 biscuits

These are just as yummy baked for breakfast and served with butter and honey as they are baked atop the casserole.

2 cups all-purpose flour
2 teaspoons baking powder
1 teaspoon baking soda
1 teaspoon salt
4 tablespoons butter, cut into 6 to 8 chunks
7/8 to 1 cup buttermilk (or 4 teaspoons powdered buttermilk and 7/8 cup water)

Pulse the dry ingredients in a food processor three to four times. Add the butter and pulse a few more times. Pour buttermilk into dry ingredients through the feed tube while pulsing; continue pulsing until the dough forms a ball. Turn the dough onto a floured board. With light, quick strokes, knead three to four times, then roll 1/2 to 3/4 inch thick and cut into desired shapes.

Bake the biscuits atop the Postholiday Turkey Casserole as described above or on a baking sheet at 425°F for 12 to 15 minutes.

High-altitude adjustment: Use only 1 teaspoon baking powder and 1/2 teaspoon baking soda.

freely—you may find that you enjoy the flavor of the fresh herb more (or less) than the dried, so adjust accordingly.

Sweet Sensations

At the other end of the culinary herbal spectrum are the so-called sweet herbs. Those used in salads or with fruit dishes include borage, burnet, hyssop, lemon balm, lemon verbena, mint, nasturtium, sweet cicely, and caraway. Some that are used in pastries, cookies, and candies include angelica, horehound, lovage, poppy seed, and anise.

If you enjoy grouping herbs by their uses, take care to make sure that their cultural requirements are met. With the sweet herbs, this is not difficult, though big brutes like angelica, lovage, or mints may overwhelm smaller companions in cramped pots.

Some herbs and edible flowers can be used strictly decoratively. It takes little time to dress up a plate with a garnish, a lovely touch that can make the "moment of presentation" a delight for guests. We serve meals on several kinds of dishes, from trea-sured Fiesta and Harlequin collections to antique and new transfer ware in several colors. The plates are pretty, and we strive to make the food on them equally attractive.

Sometimes we cradle a cold salad in kale leaves or dress it up with edible flowers such as nasturtiums, chives, roses, violets, or pot marigolds. Even though it's not particularly inventive, we use Italian parsley to garnish spicy dishes, intending to eat it at the end of the meal. Really. It seems to diminish garlic breath.

Variegated leaves, such as those of the nasturtium 'Alaska' or 'Tricolor' garden sage, look great against the shiny bright glazes of Fiesta ware. Sprigs of blooming rosemary, thyme, oregano, and savory may frame the main course on the plate. For special occasions, use satin ribbon to tie bunches of pinks, sweet Williams, bachelor's-buttons, and other flowers to decorate trays of hors d'oeuvres or tuck into guests' napkins. It takes only a few moments to raid the garden for these special touches; having attractive garnishes close at hand makes it that much easier.

POPPY-SEED CAKE
Makes one 8-inch layer cake

This dessert is the perfect ending for a meal featuring herbs. To bring out the delicious flavor of the poppy seeds, crush or grind them after soaking.

Cake
1/3 cup poppy seeds
3/4 cup milk
3/4 cup butter or margarine
1 1/2 cups sugar
1 1/2 teaspoons vanilla
2 cups sifted cake flour
1/4 teaspoon salt
2 teaspoons baking powder
4 egg whites
Custard Filling (below)
4 tablespoons powdered sugar

Soak the seeds in the milk for one hour.

Preheat the oven to 350°F. Grease and flour two 8-inch cake pans.

Cream the butter and sugar until fluffy. Add the vanilla. Sift the flour, salt, and baking powder. Add the flour mixture in three parts, alternating with thirds of the milk and poppy seeds and mixing well after each addition.

Beat the egg whites until stiff but not dry. Stir 1/2 cup of the egg whites into the batter, then gently fold in the remainder. Pour the batter into the prepared cake pans. Bake 25 minutes or until a toothpick inserted in the center of the cake comes out clean.

Remove the pans from the oven and let stand 10 minutes, then turn the cakes out onto racks and allow to cool completely.

Slice each cake in two horizontally and spread custard filling on three of the four layers. Stack the custard-covered layers and place the remaining layer on top, cut side down. Chill. Just before serving, dust the top with confectioners' sugar.

High-altitude adjustment: Reduce the sugar by 2 tablespoons and the baking powder by 1 teaspoon and add 2 more tablespoons of flour.

Custard Filling

1/2 cup sugar
1 tablespoon cornstarch
1 1/2 cups milk
4 slightly beaten egg yolks
1/2 tablespoon butter or margarine
1 teaspoon vanilla
1/4 cup chopped walnuts or pecans

Stir together the sugar and cornstarch. In a saucepan, combine the milk and egg yolks. Whisk in the sugar mixture and cook, stirring, over medium heat until the mixture comes to a boil. Off heat, stir in the butter, cool slightly, then stir in the vanilla and nuts.

CHAPTER 3
THE UNINHIBITED HERB

NOT EVERYBODY UNDERSTANDS OUR garden. People who don't garden often remain mystified by our rampaging riot of plants. People who garden in a different style may not like ours, but at least they have a feeling about it. We host many garden tours, mainly for charity, and we're often amused by visitors' reactions. "Well, I like most of it," one woman opined to her friend as Rob eavesdropped from an open window, "but this patio—all these pots—I just don't get it."

That's okay. Not everyone needs to understand our compulsion to try every plant we can get our hands on, or try to imagine what's in our heads at planting time. We could claim it's pure unadulterated artistic impulse instead of an explosion of pent-up winter frustration.

Our real motive is to create a brand new world for the season, populated by favorite old plants and new treasures brought home from friends and travels. It's a world made from pots and plants, designed to serve as a setting for our summer vacation outside.

We live outdoors most of the summer, using as our rooms our various patios, some in shade and some in sun. Summer is all too brief; if Smith and Hawken made teak beds, we'd even sleep outside. The outdoor rooms are designed just as seriously as the ones in the house; potted plants give them character. The plants may be appreciated individually or in combination, like the books, paintings, and furniture of any indoor room. Our lofty goal is a design for living.

Prints of dogs playing poker and tubs of scarlet geraniums don't need explanations; they are what they are. But fine art and fine gardening, which have quite a bit in common, rely on the context of experience to be fully appreciated. The design of a pot of

Basil, Agastache rupestris, *and burgundy fountain grass create a riot of texture, color, and flavor.*

gorgeous plants, reaching out in every direction succeeds because it suggests movement, employs contrasts of foliage size and texture, different shapes, harmonious colors—all artful notions that can be discussed as one would discuss a Matisse or a Renoir. Good design bears discussion and a depth of understanding—but after all, we're talking about plants. If one dies, or we don't like the arrangement, we change the pots around. And when all else fails, there's always a new season ahead.

DESIGNING MEN: CREATIVE HERBAL CONTAINERS

Not everybody wants a jungle; some people prefer a single painting on the wall rather than dozens of pieces hung there. But the single painting should be one that you really enjoy, as should the single pot.

The pot and its inhabitant play nearly equal roles and should suit one another. Spiky plants seem to need weighty, solid containers. A bold agave seems to demand a simple, tapered terra-cotta pot or perhaps a rounded, glazed bowl. New Zealand flax,

Some people leave Ali Baba pots empty as a restrained artistic statement, but we'd never do that, not when we could jam a plant in there.

aloes, yuccas, lemongrass, and rushes are effective as single large specimens when placed in containers that complement their open, linear habits.

Large shrubs, palms, or castor beans need stable, heavy containers not only for aesthetic reasons but to keep the wind from knocking them over. Large bay, juniper, rosemary, or box standards or other topheavy topiaries often seem perfectly stable until a strong gust catches them, flings them to the ground, and ruins their prim, manicured look.

Some argue that, for visual balance, the height of a plant should be double that of the pot. We disagree. A statuesque Ali Baba pot looks wonderful with simple succulent rosettes atop its rim, a pompom of clipped rue or santolina, a headdress of ferns or euphorbia, or the fine texture of spilling thyme. Some people leave Ali Baba pots empty as a restrained artistic statement, but we'd never do that, not when we could jam a plant in there.

As focal points or highlights to architecture, visually arresting single specimens can draw attention under an archway or inside

A potted rue, sage, fancy-leaf geranium, and peppers anchor a clump of blue oat grass.

an alcove. Matched pairs of single specimens draw attention to gates, stairs, windows, and doors.

Good candidates include plants with large, bold foliage or architectural structure such as ginger, New Zealand flax, elephant's-ear, euphorbias, palms, bananas, citrus, bay, oleander, *Angelica gigas*, ferns, junipers, or clipped box. Fine-textured herbs such as fennel, lavender, santolinas, rue, artemisias, catmints, Mexican bush sage, Russian sage, and agastaches can also be effective as single specimens if the plant is full, bushy, and set off by its pot.

People who garden strictly in containers because they lack a plot of land can enjoy handsome perennial herbs on decks, balconies, or rooftops. Tansy, bee balm, lovage, angelica, hyssop, verbascum, and yarrow can be more interesting as single

Restraint—we're not known for it, but we appreciate it.

specimens than when they are grouped in a garden.

MIX 'N' MATCH: CREATING MIXED POTS

Some gardeners like to keep their specimens separate, growing them in individual pots and grouping the pots to create combinations. Others enjoy the challenge of mixing plants in a single large container. We do both.

Creating a successful mixed pot can be a challenging and rewarding experience. If the plants look good together in a shopping cart, they'll probably look great combined in a single pot. They must share the same cultural requirements to thrive there, but their looks make them interesting companions.

Successful mixed pots rely on great foliage plants such as Helichrysum *'Limelight,' lungwort, ivy, Japanese rush, variegated myrtle, and Cuban oregano.*

In the container garden, foliage is the first consideration, as it is in our other gardens. Flowers come and go, but leaves provide constant interest throughout the season. They may be smooth, slender ones or fuzzy, flat ones. They may be green, bronze, silver, gold, or variegated. Cramming every sort of foliage type together, however, yields a planting that looks like kitchen leftovers. Starting with a theme based on foliage color—gray or bronze, for example—goes a long way toward achieving harmony in the grouping

The second consideration is shape. Upright plants often look pleasing with rounded masses at their feet and sprawling or trailing plants to fill out the composition. Putting herbs together in pots is a lot like flower arranging except that the plants grow and change after they've been arranged. Variety in shape ensures visual interest in the arrangement.

Color is less important to us than foliage and shape. Gray leaves bring out the best in pastel-toned flowers; sometimes we let silver-leaved flowering herbs dictate the color theme, such as lavender or yellow-flowered curry plant (*Helichrysum italicum*). The silveriness of gray leaves varies; some look like gray cashmere, others nearly like white felt, while still others gleam like metal. The flower colors that go with them vary as well. Deep burgundy, magenta, and rich blue or purple blossoms often show up much better in the company of silver foliage than they would against a backdrop of plain green; the softer silver color does not compete with the intensity of the blooms.

Bronze- and purple-leaved plants invite more adventuresome combinations with deep purple or smoldering red and orange tones. Golden or chartreuse leaves have such a strong presence that they contrast effectively with the brilliant jewel tones of hot pink, magenta, orange, blue, and purple. We often feature variegated foliage as the main attraction, downplaying the colors of its floral accompaniments by selecting companions with small blossoms or short bloom periods.

When planting time comes, however, we often ignore principles of color and foliage

Deep burgundy, magenta, and rich blue or purple blossoms often show up much better in the company of silver foliage than they would against a backdrop of plain green.

Canna, abutilon, and the Oriental lily 'Garden Party' combine for a lavish group of containers.

Every plant counts—here, a tiny scented geranium complements the bulk of a striped canna.

use and follow whatever muse is working that day. Sometimes it's a muse with a really twisted sense of aesthetics.

STAGE CRAFT: PLACING POTS

Although it's possible to arrange a pleasing combination of pots of various sizes on the ground, the effect is heightened—literally—when the pots are brought up to eye level or above. Anyone who's ever stacked a board-and-brick bookcase can make similar bleachers for plants. For grander effect, some gardeners rely on iron baker's racks, Victorian-style tiered stands, or pedestals. Drainage tiles and chimney flues of different lengths also make creatively staged planters.

As the centerpiece of a grouping, we usually start with a bold foliage plant such as the variegated, yellow-and-green-striped *Canna* 'Pretoria'. This stunning orange-flowered plant actually performs better in a pot of compost-enriched, moisture-retentive soil than it does in our beds of fast-draining sandy loam. Joining the canna is a pot of cream-margined variegated *Abutilon* 'Souvenir de Bonn' with dusky orange blossoms. The crowning glory of the arrangement is a dozen bulbs of the Oriental lily 'Garden Party', a compact grower with fragrant gold-banded white flowers.

More plants with variegated foliage seem logical for the ensemble, so we add the scented geranium 'Atomic Snowflake' along with variegated Cuban oregano (*Plectranthus amboinicus*) and nasturtium 'Alaska'. We also keep in mind leaf shapes, the exact color of variegation, and its distribution on the leaf. The chartreuse-leaved sweet potato vine 'Marguerite' and a pot of fine-textured southernwood play up all that over-the-top variegation. That's one of the pleasures of container gardening: making outrageous horticultural statements. If you don't like what they say, edit out the parts that don't work by moving a pot or two.

Any bold plant can serve as a point of departure. Instead of a canna, try a palm, banana, aloe, or a large specimen of Jerusalem sage, artemisia, or lavender. Build around it, adding complementary and contrasting plants. Take a break and get away from it for a while, then take a fresh look to see what works and what doesn't.

GRACING THE GARDEN: POTS IN THE BORDERS

We're unenthusiastic about most garden sculpture, or at least the sculpture we can

A heavy, solid pot of colorful annual flowers anchors each end of our long, frothy borders, providing a pleasing contrast to fine-textured perennials.

afford. Nonetheless, people have presented us with cast-concrete sculptures of all sorts, which we've reluctantly set in dim, shady places. If a visitor makes the mistake of admiring one—or even acknowledging it by saying something like "Oh, look at the dragon"— we immediately insist that she should have it. We don't take no for an answer and lug it immediately to her car.

Despite our distaste for cast-concrete critters, we acknowledge that some parts of the garden need a focal point. A pot can fill the bill. Its simple, pleasing shape draws the eye to stairs, an entry, or other architectural form. Such a pot may be placed directly in the garden, as a centerpiece to a bed or a component of a border.

A heavy, solid pot of colorful annual flowers anchors each end of our long, frothy borders, providing a pleasing contrast to fine-textured perennials such as baby's-breath, catmints, thread-leaf coreopsis, and tunic flower (*Petrorhagia saxifraga*). Especially effective in the pot are bold-leaved herbs such as *Plectranthus argentatus*, castor bean, or sweet potato vine.

Adding a pot of New Zealand flax,

A pot of kale, sage, and licorice plants admirably fills a bare spot in the autumn border.

Artemisia 'Powis Castle,' or sage to an awkward bare spot transforms the eyesore into an asset. A pot may even be wriggled into an apparently full border—gently pull the overgrown plants apart and see whether there's enough space between them.

Potted herbs can play off the linear textures of grasses or yuccas growing in the ground. Blue oat grass makes a splendid backdrop for a stout pot filled with the pleasantly contrasting foliage of lady's-mantle, golden variegated sage, rue, scented geraniums, and ornamental peppers. To complement the broad yellow stripes of *Yucca filamentosa*, we use pots of lime green-foliaged *Helichrysum petiolare* 'Limelight' and gray-and-yellow-leaved 'Variegatum', golden oregano, golden feverfew, and yellow-flowered santolina, rue, *Coreopsis* 'Moonbeam', and marigolds.

Helichrysum '*Limelight*', Plectranthus argentatus, *canna, and dusty miller overflow their pot to join the border.*

Pots of good-looking foliage herbs such as perilla, *Salvia officinalis* 'Berggarten', and scented geraniums also complement blossoms of the moment: spring peonies, summer phlox, fall asters. Mature potted specimens of chard, kale, or sage give a fresh look to the autumnal garden while concealing the bare spots resulting from pulling out the perennials that haven't lived up to our standards.

Weather and watering eventually take their toll on most objects that weren't designed to hold plants. Don't ruin a family heirloom for the sake of basil and also consider whether the planter will be truly charming or simply tacky.

canisters, wastebaskets. Leaky ones may even have adequate drainage without drilling additional holes in the bottom. Decorative old cracker, biscuit, or olive oil tins make great groupings. Tea tins— we have dozens—are just large enough to support young herb plants. We add drain holes, pop in rooted cuttings of thyme, sage, and other tough Mediterranean herbs, and display them on an east-facing windowsill. The hot western sun can bake the roots of plants set in tiny metal tins.

PERSONAL PREFERENCE: UNUSUAL HERBAL CONTAINERS

Gardening is about personal expression. Not simply content to grow their herbs in plain old pots or boxes, some gardeners employ all sorts of quirky containers. For some reason we can't fathom, many look to the bottom of their closets, stuffing old boots and shoes with hen-and-chickens or thyme. If the shoe fits, they'll plant it.

Rummaging through the basement, garage, attic, or shed turns up many candidates for whimsical containers: buckets, coal scuttles, cast-iron kettles, washtubs, kitchen

The sky's the limit when it comes to glass, porcelain, and pottery containers. Crocks, teapots, mixing bowls, umbrella stands, and anything else that can hold soil are at risk of becoming container gardens. They don't breathe like terra-cotta, so they're not ideal for every plant. A fine masonry bit comes in handy when drilling drainage holes. It's risky and sometimes results in disaster, but all is not lost: a few of our friends glue the broken bits of old dishes onto standard clay pots, creating one-of-a-kind mosaics.

Nearly any gardener can rustle up a pleasing assortment of wooden bushel baskets, nail casks, barrels, butter churns, trunks, chests, and shop projects gone wrong. We've used wine and fruit crates with good results. The bottoms of bushel baskets will rot out after a few years, but they look great in an informal setting, such as around a potting shed. For whimsy, why not plant an old milk box with milk thistle?

Tightly woven wicker baskets also fall into the category of short-lived containers. And don't forget straw hats, fishing creels, picnic baskets, and clothes hampers. Besides being fun, wicker containers have great drainage.

Weather and watering eventually take their toll on most objects that weren't designed to hold plants. Don't ruin a family heirloom for the sake of basil and also consider whether the planter will be truly charming or simply tacky. We've got an old set of suitcases with a fake alligator finish that might make an interesting planted grouping for a bon voyage party, but they would become tiresome over the long term. We can even picture a tree festooned with dozens of hanging handbag planters, but the neighbors think we're peculiar enough as it is. Some people enjoy challenging the world with their personal statements; maybe the urge to perch purses in your pear tree shouldn't be thwarted.

Our friend Susan amassed a collection of

A rosemary topiary takes a seat in the vegetable garden.

Gardens are personal places and often repositories for found objects and mementos.

iron, tin, stone, and glass castoffs from farming, mining, and ranching that find new uses in her very personal garden. A former terrazzo washbasin from an elementary school (you stepped on a foot lever to make water spurt from a perforated pipe on top) became a unique water garden that supports cattails, rushes, doku-dami, and water hyacinths along with a family of goldfish.

Certain furniture and appliances are quite appealing as planters. We'd draw the line at bathroom commodes but have no strong objections to a claw-footed tub foaming with herbs; it's one way to keep soapwort (*Saponaria officinalis*) from taking over the garden and a subtle nod to the tradition of using the leaves to produce a soapy lather for washing.

We found one our favorite pieces of furniture-turned-planter in our friend Nancy's garden, a wooden chair with its caned seat long gone. The hole is just the right size to hold a standard plastic hanging basket. (Fiddling with the S-hooks and wire can adjust the basket to a larger or smaller opening.) A bit of moss hides the rim.

We leave the wagon wherever it looks best for a week or so at a time, and sometimes we wheel it in front of a moth-eaten part of the border.

Thyme, sage, and society garlic are sitting pretty in the new seat.

With a bit of ingenuity, our friend Rosie has enclosed junked iron bed frames with cement blocks and filled them with soil. With a fresh coat of fresh white paint, these are the prettiest, wittiest "flower beds" imaginable, filled as they are with patchwork quilts of flowers, fruit, and foliage.

Movable containers put herbs on the go. A wheelbarrow—the older and leakier the better—makes a super planter. When our old wheelbarrow got too wobbly and leaky, we parked it by the potting shed, shoveled in some fresh compost, and planted it with tough plants that would thrive without much fuss. Yarrows, daylilies, sages, coreopsis, liatris, and thymes turned an old piece of junk into a focal point in a neglected part of the garden.

We can imagine several other movable containers. An old cart or wagon—ceramic burro optional—would look great holding a profusion of plants. An old soapbox derby car could put zip into a planting. We've seen worn-out rowboats and canoes converted into planters; a former crib or baby buggy might find the same use. Might we suggest a centerpiece of baby's-breath? Baby's-tears? Baby-blue-eyes? Should we stop now?

When we found a beat-up child's wagon at a flea market, we put it to use hauling plants from the car to the garden. The flat bed, enclosed by the classic red railings, accommodated many more plants than a wheelbarrow without risk of tipping, and the pots looked attractive in it. Now, after the spring rush, we use it as a movable planter.

Catmints, grasses, sages, yarrows, Cuban oregano, basils, perilla, and castor beans have been part of the movable feast. We leave the wagon wherever it looks best for a week or so at a time, pulling it out of the way for mowing. Sometimes we wheel it in front of a moth-eaten part of the border to distract the attention of visitors.

We haul plants in this old wagon in the spring, but the rest of the season it holds cannas, catmint, perilla, bronze fennel, and castor bean.

CHAPTER 4
SPECIAL INTERESTS

TOPIARIES EVOKE THE LONG-GONE Victorian era—a time of unlimited gardening help for the wealthy, public parks with amazing plantings, and huge glasshouses. Today, only a few large public gardens can put on the kind of displays that we've seen in old garden books. Further, most gardeners have no interest in creating huge topiary birds sitting on nests or green versions of Barney the Dinosaur frolicking amid the perennial beds. Nonetheless, we appreciate the elegant beauty of potted topiaries, but recognize that those of any size they require a good deal of time and attention in their development and maintenance, which would cut into our other gardening pleasures. So we restrain ourselves from getting carried away.

A surprising number of herbs make fine candidates for topiary. The best are perennials that produce a woody stem that can be trained. Some annual herbs have perennial counterparts with woody stems, such as 'African Blue' basil, but make sure your investigations include a taste test if you enjoy using the herb for cooking.

The classic lollipop standards are among the easiest topiaries to create and maintain.

Good candidates for this type of topiary include scented geraniums, bay, sages, santolinas, lavenders, lemon verbena, boxwoods, junipers, flowering maples, citrus, myrtle, and rosemaries. Other herbs that might not ordinarily come to mind for this purpose can also be trained easily: golden marjoram (*Origanum vulgare* 'Aureum'); heliotrope; helichrysums; and dense, upright honeysuckles such as *Lonicera nitida* 'Baggesen's Gold'). We've also seen interesting thyme topiaries created by weaving several long stems together to form the trunk. They look like miniature versions of the common woven houseplant, *Ficus benjamina*.

Start your topiary with a plant that's about two years old (or a strong cutting with well-established roots) and an established central leader. If you're growing the plant from seed, begin early to pinch off shoots around the lower two-thirds of the main leader. Tie the main leader to a bamboo stake to help keep it straight and upright; this will become the topiary's "trunk." Pinch off most of the lower leaves and side branches, leaving only a tuft of leaves at the top. The height of the crown of foliage at the top of the central leader should be one-third to one-quarter of the height of the entire topiary when training is complete; keep this general rule in mind as you pinch away side branches.

Select a well-drained pot about 2 inches in diameter larger than the plant's root ball and elevate it slightly to encourage drainage. As your plant grows, it will need repotted; the larger the plant, the more critical it becomes to avoid narrow, tall pots that can't balance the top-heavy topiary. When the plant reaches maturity, you may wish to tip the plant from its pot, carefully remove any loose soil, and return it to its pot with fresh soil.

Be careful not to damage the growing tip at the top of the central leader. When the plant has reached the desired height, pinch out the tip. The plant's energy will then be directed to the branches of the crown; they will grow more swiftly than before. As the crown develops, shape it into a ball with regular, symmetrical trimming, which promotes branching of the stems.

The larger the plant, the more critical it becomes to avoid narrow, tall pots that can't balance the top-heavy topiary.

People who like poodles can try their hand at creating a topiary with two or three balls on a single stem. This takes time and frequent pinching below the crown until the stem has reached a suitable height. At that point, remove the growing tip and allow one or two sets of side shoots to grow out at regular intervals along the trunk. With practice, it's possible to create even more than three pom-poms. Other shapes—cones and so on—are fashioned in the same manner.

Many standards try to cloak their naked stems with side shoots; keep removing them. Three or more standards planted side by side in a long pot may be trained into a miniature Belgian fence by allowing the crowns to grow together or by training side branches into diagonal patterns. But how much time do you have on your hands?

A circular rosemary topiary frames several others of varying plants and sizes.

A local greenhouse that specializes in herb topiaries has a plaque on the wall that reads, "A pinch a day—that's the topiary way." This ideal maintenance regimen isn't practical; frequent attention is required to keep topiaries in good condition. Because the symmetry of a topiary is important, turn the plant frequently so that all sides receive enough sunlight, an especially important concern for topiaries kept indoors on a windowsill or in a sunroom. We've ended up with some pretty lopsided topiaries, even outdoors. We once forgot about a santolina set against the house, and it never did straighten up. Obviously, we're not cut out to grow topiaries on a grand scale.

FALSE TOPIARY

It's far more difficult to clip a plant into the shape of a peacock than it is to create the shape of a peacock from wire and grow a plant over it. False topiaries aren't pruned into shape; the preordained form of a bunny, kitty, or teddy bear is simply covered up with an accommodating vine or creeping ivy, rosemary, or fig (*Ficus pumila*). Sometimes the stems of the plant are wrapped around the form and secured with a discreet twist-tie or "hairpin" of floral wire, taking advantage of the plant's twining habit or the flexibility of its youthful stems.

Lonicera *'Baggeson's Gold' takes shape as a garden guardian.*

A santolina topiary that would turn a poodle green with envy takes more than a "pinch a day," but yields striking results.

Forms constructed of chicken wire may be stuffed with sphagnum moss. Creeping plants thrust their roots into the moist moss, but the trick is to keep the moss damp. Otherwise, the plant will refuse to cover the entire structure or show unsightly brown patches. You've probably seen mangy reindeer topiaries that dried out too many times and never became the fluffy green creatures their owners envisioned. These topiaries are more successfully developed in humid climates, and even then they need frequent thorough soakings and regular watering, too.

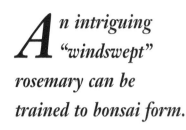

An intriguing "windswept" rosemary can be trained to bonsai form.

BONSAI

Though bonsai comes from Oriental rather than European gardening tradition, it bears some similarities to topiary. Both techniques require patience and pruning. The art of bonsai (which we don't practice, by the way) seeks to draw out the beauty of a particular plant by years of meticulous training that produce a miniature version of a mature specimen sculpted by nature. Some bonsai specimens have been passed from generation to generation over several hundred years.

Herbs don't live that long, of course, and in comparison they grow speedily. Woody rosemaries, junipers, lemon verbena, dwarf citrus, and sages lend themselves to bonsai training most readily. Start with a plant that displays an unusual or intriguing shape, such as a "windswept" rosemary. The idea is to prune away superfluous growth to expose the stem, bark, and the most elegant branches. Balanced pruning of the greenery and the roots keeps the plant compact. Restricting the plant to a small container and withholding fertilizer also slows development. Wire is often used to train the main stem into the desired shape and direction.

Some bonsai growers in mild climates keep their plants outdoors year-round, but plants in small pots are extremely vulnerable to frost. Bonsai plants also need constant attention to watering: one hot, dry weekend can wipe out an entire collection. When you vacation, don't leave your bonsai in the hands of an absent-minded friend. In fact, if you get serious about bonsai, you may never vacation again.

Mastering bonsai takes years; we recommend that those interested in the art consult books on the subject; in some areas, bonsai groups meet regularly and hold classes.

Hanging baskets, such as these filled with licorice plant, fuchsias, petunias, and impatiens are especially elegant when seen against a dark background of evergreens.

Hanging Baskets: New Heights

Hanging baskets bring herbs close to kitchens, sitting areas, or entryways. Some gardeners prefer the ease of planting a plastic or clay pot, while others start with a wire frame and sphagnum moss. Plastic is lightweight and slows the evaporation of water from the soil. Terra-cotta adds weight and allows fairly rapid evaporation. An arrangement of wire and sphagnum moss offers design opportunities that the others do not and weighs very little, but it requires frequent watering. In dry climates, some gardeners add a thin layer of plastic sheeting between the moss and soil to slow evaporation, making four or five slits an inch or two long in the plastic.

Whichever type of basket you select, however, go for it with gusto by choosing plants that will tumble and cascade over its edges. Too many hanging baskets are planted with unsuitable, upright-growing plants that will never spill over the sides in billowing cascades. When we use plastic, we opt for white or terra-cotta-colored ones instead of that awful green shade that upstages every green found in nature.

Wire-and-moss baskets can accommodate trailing plants set directly into the sides of the container, whereas standard plastic baskets can be planted only in the top. A wire basket is first lined with thoroughly dampened moss and then filled with moist soil. Don't put moss on the top of the soil. With your fingers, make a hole in the moss and the underlying soil that is just wide enough to stuff in a plant's root ball. Depending on the mature size of the plant, insert a plant every 4 or 5 inches; on top, you can set plants closer together. If using plastic sheeting, cut small slits to slip the root balls through to the soil.

We like our hanging baskets to look lush fast, so we start with large transplants and include fast-growing trailing herbs such as variegated ground ivy (*Glechoma hederacea* 'Variegata'), plectranthus such as *Plectranthus forsteri* 'Marginatus', licorice plant, ivy, dead nettle, or periwinkle. Creeping thymes usually don't grow long enough to conceal the sides of the basket fully, so they may be planted along with a more vigorously trailing plant.

Prostrate rosemary, savories, dianthus, golden marjoram, and wall germander (*Teucrium chamaedrys*) trail effectively from a basket. The charming shrimplike flowers of dittany of Crete (*Origanum dictamnus*) or Lebanese oregano (*O. libanoticum*) show to best advantage dangling from a basket. Garden sage also sprawls out attractively. Geraniums with scents such as old spice, nutmeg, and peppermint also work well. We once saw a London pub with deep green faux marble exterior walls accented by cascades of gleaming orange and yellow nasturtium flowers—an unforgettable sight.

Other candidates to intermingle with herbs in baskets include lobelia (*Lobelia erinus* cultivars), lantanas, verbenas, trailing petunias, tickseed (*Bidens* spp.), fuchsias, black-eyed Susan vine (*Thunbergia alata*), and sweet alyssum.

For foliage contrast, consider the highly ornamental sweet potato vines: maroon 'Blackie', variegated 'Tricolor', or chartreuse 'Margarita'. Variegated apple mint is especially pretty in concert with ivy geraniums and chartreuse 'Limelight' licorice plant. The dark bronze-red leaves and pendant coral blossoms of 'Gartenmeister Bonstedt' fuschia cascade dramatically from the top of a basket add fire to these herbs. The finely cut silver leaves and scarlet blooms of parrot's-beak along with the bright green asparagus fern make excellent foils for these herbs as well. Upright herbs such as chives or society garlic may be included in a basket, but avoid tall, stiff ones that make the design look top-heavy.

Many people make the mistake of hanging their baskets too high; instead, place them so that you can enjoy your basket at eye level and water it easily. Experience has taught us to wrap a twist-tie around the point at which the basket's hook contacts the support hook to secure the basket lest high winds slip it off and send it crashing to earth.

WINDOW BOXES: FRAMING THE VIEW

Not every window box sits or hangs at the base of a window. Planter boxes also serve handsomely on decks, porches, and patios. Their long, narrow shape works where round pots don't fit—atop walls, on narrow steps, hanging from deck railings, or setting the boundaries for an outdoor living space. Perhaps the most obvious use of a planter box is to beautify a window from both sides.

Many herb lovers appreciate simple pleasures, such as the breeze coming through an open window at suppertime. If there's a window box just outside, we can reach out and pinch a few sprigs of basil or parsley or just enjoy their pleasant scents and colors. Seen from the other side of the window, the herbs and flowers tumbling from boxes give the home a friendly look, complementing and softening the house's exterior for the summer. In winter, the box can be planted with salad greens and pot marigolds in warm-winter climates. Where winters are long and cold, they can be filled with arrangements of rose hips and dried flowers or branches of holly, ivy, conifers, and winterberry. We eschew plastic poinsettias, however, and urge others to do the same.

Perennial herbs that ordinarily live through the winter in the ground in your area may not survive in a box due to the

Mixed window boxes and topiary soften a brick staircase.

A terra-cotta box teams with Mexican bush sage, miniature roses, flowering maples, and geraniums.

stress of alternately freezing and thawing, as well as desiccation by wind and sun. You may increase their chance of survival by removing them from the boxes in late autumn and planting them in a trench. Then protect them with a mulch of evergreen boughs or straw.

By the end of winter, most window boxes hold only forlorn remnants of the past year's glory—a few tan wisps of asparagus fern and maybe some freeze-dried petunias. Spring weather, however, inspires combinations of primroses, parsley, cilantro, English daisy, mustard, arugula, chervil, salad greens, stocks, pansies, and other plants that revel in cool temperatures and can withstand a few degrees of frost.

As the spring bloomers begin to suffer from the heat, replace them with summer stalwarts. Informal plantings are easy to patch up if a plant or two dies or is damaged. One neighbor found that vandals had toppled her box from the porch during the night. She wrestled it back into place, scooped her impatiens, Madagascar periwinkle, and Johnny-jump-ups from the sidewalk, and hurriedly

*W*here winters are long and cold, fill window boxes with arrangements of rose hips and dried flowers or branches of holly, ivy, conifers, and winterberry.

replanted them. That box looked even better the second time around.

Later in the summer, add kale, coneflowers, ruby chard, mums, asters, and late-blooming sages to the mix. A changing window box gives a fresh look to a house quicker and more cheaply than a new coat of paint. Window boxes are also ideal for compulsive shoppers who feel drawn to the nursery every few weeks.

Place a box near a window or on the patio to attract butterflies or hummingbirds. Good bets to draw them include members of the carrot family such as dill, fennel, and Queen-Anne's-lace, which are food sources for caterpillars of swallowtail butterflies. The flowers of scabious, bee balm, verbena (*Lantana camara* cultivars), lion's-ear (*Leonotus leonurus*), and numerous sages, among others, attract butterflies. Hummingbirds go for the red tubular flowers of beard-tongue (*Penstemon barbatus*), bee balm, cardinal flower (*Lobelia cardinalis*), autumn sage *Salvia greggii*, Texas sage (*S. coccinea*), and pineapple sage, but they also visit flowers that are neither red nor tubular. Look around your garden

A sturdy carpenter's box carries licorice plant, society garlic, Mexican bush sage, Cuban oregano, lemongrass, and bronze-leaf Euphorbia dulcis *'Chameleon'*.

HERBS IN POTS

to observe which plants attract the butterflies and hummingbirds, then fill your window boxes with the most popular ones. Finally, sit back and enjoy the show.

Freestanding wicker window boxes, once popular fixtures in American homes, can still be found in antique or second-hand stores. A fresh coat of white or traditional dark green paint restores their good looks. An advantage of these old boxes, which originally held a metal liner to protect the wicker from moisture, is that they may be positioned inside or out; they're as striking on a porch or balcony as in the dining room.

If you spy an old carpenter's box, an open wooden box with a dowel handle on top, you can convert it into an appealing planter. Such boxes may fit on windowsills or benches and are somewhat portable, depending on your strength.

Window boxes are intended to frame the view, and herbs and companion flowers with rounded or tight, upright shapes fill the bill. These include many scented geraniums, basil, heliotrope, rue, coleus, peppers, perilla, eggplant, miniature roses, sage, and lavender. Tall plants can get in the way, but the wispy spikes of *Verbena bon-*

If you plan to build a window box, consider this: a cubic foot of soil weighs from 50 to 90 pounds. We did not learn this by playing Trivial Pursuit.

ariensis, pineapple sage, or dill can be a delightful see-through component.

Upright spiky herbs add spark. Society garlic (*Tulbaghia violacea*), chives, garlic chives, lemongrass, and Mexican bush sage suggest shooting fireworks above the major plantings. Trailing and sprawling plants provide a lush, cascading look that we see in most successful window boxes. Ivy, Cuban oregano, licorice plant (*Helichrysum petiolare* cultivars), savories, dianthus, prostrate rosemary, Madagascar periwinkle, dead nettle (*Lamium maculatum*), parrot's-beak (*Lotus berthelotii*), thyme, creeping oregano, and moneywort (*Lysimachia nummularia*) are good foliage spillers.

For a dash of colorful flowers, insert dianthus, trailing verbenas, catmint, dwarf lantana, tuberous begonias, or nasturtiums. Cherry tomatoes bred for hanging baskets add cheerful spots of color.

Vines such as hops or morning glory usually don't spill, since their inclination is to clamber up the box's other inhabitants, but if the other herbs can handle the load, they can be effective.

Most herbs perform admirably in win-

Densely planted cascading nasturtiums, licorice plant, ivies, impatiens, petunias, and geraniums conceal their container.

dow boxes when their cultural requirements of light, soil, and fertilizer are met. Because they are exposed to a bit more wind than containers on the ground and in some cases also to the reflected heat of masonry, the boxes must be kept evenly moist for their contents to grow as rambunctiously as we'd like.

If you plan to build a window box, consider this: a cubic foot of soil weighs from 50 to 90 pounds. We did not learn this by playing Trivial Pursuit but by building wooden planter boxes. Although we had fun with our project, we recommend that you consult a book on household carpentry projects before beginning. Make sure the book you choose deals specifically with ways of supporting the weight of both box and soil and methods of controlling the water that will drain from the pots inside.

Wooden planter boxes offer several advantages. The insulating value of wood keeps the soil relatively cool and moist, so that the box needs watering only every three or four days, depending on how much sun the plants receive. Cleats or blocks that raise the bottom of the box off the ground or deck prevent damage to wooden porches and keep the bottom of the box from rotting.

A window box, however, needs drainage holes and caulked seams to prevent water stains on the side of the house and cork or wooden spacers to keep the box from direct contact with the house siding, further

TIPS FOR SUCCESSFUL WINDOW BOXES

- Location, location, location—choose the right plants for the location. Most culinary herbs need at least half a day of full sun and can survive, with sufficient water, the blasts of sun on southern and western exposures. Some herbs need protection or thrive in shade.
- Fertilize the plants consistently with a balanced, general formula fertilizer. Lack of root nourishment can cause the midsummer blahs.
- Use no pesticides stronger than soap. Dishwashing liquid makes an effective solution to use in treating minor insect infestations; insecticidal soap is better.
- Don't put up with boring. If the herbs in your window box aren't producing pizzazz, pull them out and replace them with others more to your liking.

NEIGHBORHOOD PORCH BOXES

Many years ago, when we lived in a turn-of-the-century row house in central Denver, we banded together with a dozen of our neighbors to brighten our porches by constructing simple planters: containers 3 feet long, 1 foot wide, and 1 foot deep.

Although cedar or redwood is ordinarily recommended for this purpose, we opted to use cheaper 2-by-12-inch construction-grade fir because most of us were students or struggling artists. We overlapped the end pieces with the 3-foot boards, rather than mitering the corners. We did not drill any drainage holes, figuring that our products would have plenty of leaks, and they did.

The boxes were constructed in a single spring afternoon. We formed a crude assembly line; some cut the lumber while others nailed the boxes together. Some boxes were painted for protection from the elements. That extra effort paid off—most of those boxes are still there nearly two decades later.

One of our neighborhood rites of spring was the planting of the boxes and the unofficial but highly competitive Best Box contest. Our household usually scored well for originality, selection of plants, and color schemes.

One totally inexperienced gardener produced colorful creations for several years. She eventually confessed to buying preplanted peat boxes from the nursery and burying them in her own under cover of darkness. When she actually took the plunge and began to put her own designs together, however, she continued to put the rest of us to shame.

Miniature varieties of hens-and-chickens come in handy for soothing insect stings and bites.

reducing the chance of moisture's rotting the shingles or clapboards.

MINIATURE GARDENS: TINY TREASURES

Limited space sometimes dictates that gardeners grow compact, space-saving cultivars and varieties of herbs and vegetables. Dwarf oreganos, thymes, and feverfews take up little room. Compact tomatoes, cucumbers, head lettuce, and even zucchini are available at garden centers and by mail. A small deck or patio and some containers can support an astonishing variety of fresh herbs and vegetables.

Tiny treasures—thimbles or miniature teacups, say—fascinate many of us. Perhaps it's a holdover from childhood, when we imagined ourselves inside a dollhouse. Rob had a tiny farm set, complete with pigs,

The secret to this microcosm of the desert is that each plant is individually potted, then sunk in sand.

sheep, and cows no bigger than pinto beans. He had plenty of other toys—most long forgotten—but those miniature farm animals linger in his mind. No wonder he turned every old fishbowl, rose bowl, and big glass jar in his mom's cupboards into a terrarium.

Almost any clear glass container can be made into a terrarium, a transparent enclosure for raising small plants. Lidded containers such as candy or large food jars create a humid environment suitable for woodland or tropical herbs such as Corsican mint, violets, gotu kola (*Centella asiatica*), creeping fig, ivy, pennyroyal, and small rushes, ferns, and palms. Some people like adding miniature figurines such as girls holding umbrellas, winsome Oriental women, or Bambi. We think that gardeners with young children have an excuse to decorate their terrariums (try dinosaurs!), but the rest of us risk a visit by the taste police.

To plant a terrarium, first sterilize the glass and add charcoal to the moistened steriile soil mix to deter souring of the soil. We add a bit of shredded sphagnum moss, as we believe it keeps down the green slime. The soil ought to be deep enough to hold the root balls of the little plants; dig a little hole for the plant and firm it in gently. Water sparingly but consistently; if moisture begins to drip down the inside of the glass, remove the lid for a couple of hours.

C losed terraria need little attention once planted, but never leave one in direct sunlight unless you wish to cook its inhabitants.

Closed terraria need little attention once planted, but never leave one in direct sunlight unless you wish to cook its inhabitants.

An open container such as a fishbowl can support a wider range of herbs than a closed terrarium and may be placed on a windowsill. Short or creeping thymes and ivies may be contrasted with clumps of hen-and-chickens and taller, vertical herbs. Young transplants of basil, sage, myrtle, and dwarf boxwood may be kept in check by vigorous pruning and a starvation diet, but eventually they will grow too large for the confines of an open terrarium. Then tear up the whole thing and start over with new plants.

A dish garden is another way to group and display collections of herbs that are small in stature or can be restricted by ruthless pruning. Candidates include creeping

German chamomile, Corsican mint, 'Spicy Globe' and red-leaved 'Mini Purpurascens Wellsweep' basil, creeping pennyroyal, smaller thymes and germanders, dwarf dianthuses such as 'Tiny Rubies', and young plants of burnet, chervil, parsley, and sage.

Small succulents such as aloes, agaves, and hen-and-chickens may be incorporated or displayed together in a dish garden of their own. Wide, shallow terra-cotta bowls or pot saucers are ideal. Perch these conversation pieces on a table on the patio or porch where they can be best appreciated.

Miniature knot gardens can add a formal touch to a small sitting area. Choose a raised planter or suitable container; a knot garden need not be square. Recreate a classic design in miniature or make up one of your own. Execute it using 2 1/4-inch pots of green and gray santolina, golden-leaved 'Golden Moss' dwarf feverfew, compact basils, wall germander, and thymes (green, golden, or variegated) set tightly together for fast fill-in.

Regular manicuring keeps the plants thick and bushy. Fertilize sparingly to keep

Wide, shallow terra-cotta bowls or pot saucers are ideal for planting small succulents such as aloes, agaves, and hen-and-chickens.

the plants from outgrowing their boundaries. Aquarium or pea gravel in different shades may be used as a mulch to accent the patterns made by the knots.

AROMATICS: POTTED POTPOURRI

We can't resist rubbing a leaf of a favorite aromatic plant between our fingers to release its perfume, especially when it's within easy reach. Scented geraniums are the undisputed favorites among scratch-'n'-sniff gardeners. A trip around the patio of an aficionado usually wears out our noses, like trying every sample bottle at the cologne counter. We favor the citrus and rose scents, but the oddball smells are intriguing, such as the so-called nutmeg, which to us smells like after-shave.

Those bracing, pungent scents don't appeal to everyone; add just a touch of sweetness, however, and it seems everyone loves the fragrance. Our potted lavender plants get fondled constantly; there are subtle distinctions between the English, Spanish, French and other types, but most visitors agree that the English lavenders

Scented geraniums tolerate mild drought, so they adapt to relatively small pots.

have the best scent. German chamomile smells like baking apples while Cuban oregano carries a spicy scent blending oregano, thyme, and menthol. For a tired gardener, a sniff of Cuban oregano is like taking smelling salts.

Some of our favorite potted plants for idle sniffing are the sages. Cleveland sage (*Salvia clevelandii*) smells like hand lotion while pineapple sage, liked by almost everyone, smells very fruity.

Mint-scented double-bubble mint (*Agastache barberi*) makes a pretty shrub 3 feet tall and nearly as wide that is covered from midsummer to fall with rose to magenta flowering spikes up to 12 inches long. The equally large, tawny-pink-flowered *A. rupestris* and its showier cultivar 'Apricot Sunrise' have foliage that combines fruit and mint fragrances.

Many gardeners value bee balm, whose scent has been described as resembling that of the bergamot orange, a small citrus plant, grown in Italy, that gives Earl Gray tea its distinctive flavor. Powdery mildew is often a problem with the red-flowered species, but cultivars such as 'Aquarius', 'Gardenview Scarlet', and 'Marshall's Delight' feature mildew resistance as well as varied blossom colors, but they're not perfect.

Coyote mint (*Monardella odoratissima*), a native of the American West, looks like a miniature bee balm, to which it is related. Only a foot tall, it carries a crown of lavender flowers atop stems bearing small gray-green leaves. The plant's fragrance is mintier than any true mint, the olfactory equivalent of popping an Altoid.

Sweet-scented herbs are most welcome on our patio. A single plant of valerian sweetens the breeze for weeks in late spring as dianthuses add spice; these usually rebloom sporadically after deadheading. Cottage pinks (*Dianthus plumarius*) have gray, pine-needle leaves and single flowers in white or shades of pink. Maiden pinks (*D. deltoides*) offer a profusion of white to shocking pink single flowers over trailing, mat-forming green leaves. Crossing

carnations with cottage pinks created the Allwood hybrids (*D. ×allwoodii*). Their thin foliage is gray; the pink, red, salmon, white, yellow, or bicolored flowers look and smell like miniature carnations and bloom most of the season if kept deadheaded. Dianthuses suffer in soggy soil; gardeners in rainy regions would do well to provide potting soil that drains rapidly.

One of our favorite summer fragrances is that of heliotrope, an annual. Its scent has often been compared to warm cherry pie. We like the compact cultivar 'Iowa' with pale lavender flowers. Because heliotrope plants grown from seed often don't have much fragrance, choose those propagated from cuttings—and sniff before you buy. If you should find a seed-grown plant with a good scent, keep it going by growing annual root cuttings

We grow several dwarf varieties of lemon and orange for their delightfully scented flowers. We don't really care if fruit follows, but it's remarkably sweet, too. Don't bother trying to germinate the seeds of supermarket fruit. This fruit comes from standard-sized trees for which few of us have space, and years will pass before you sniff a single flower.

THE MEDICINE POT: HERBS FOR HEALTH

Many healing plants possess no outstanding ornamental qualities, but we forgive them because of their medicinal properties. Some don't take to growing in pots, especially some of the woodland herbs of America such as goldenseal. Trees and shrubs with healing properties, such as yew, aren't ordinarily grown in containers, but nothing is impossible.

Perennial herbs with traditions of healing can thrive in pots; these include lungwort, St.-John's-wort, motherwort, boneset, Madagascar periwinkle, gotu kola, and comfrey, not to mention feverfew, foxglove, milk thistle, chamomile, mint, clary sage, valerian, and echinacea. We don't recommend, of course, that gardeners nibble indiscriminately among their potted healing herbs; if you'd like to use medicinal herbs, do your homework to learn whether you should take them, and then how to prepare them.

Nearly everyone can enjoy the herbs used creams, lotions, soaps, liniments, and bath teas. Sage, lavender, and eucalyptus are among these low-risk herbs.

We've made the mistake of buying so-called potpourri that isn't much more than stained wood chips and strawflowers doused with sweet-scented oil. The real thing—made from roses, lavender, costmary, scented geraniums and such—is infinitely better. Sleep pillows, lavender wands, and pomades make our house smell as though Shakers live here. It reeks of industriousness and wholesomeness, even when

Lavender smells delicious, and its essential oil has long been used on minor burns.

*The turquoise foliage of rue, artemisia, and succulents contrast with
fragrant Oriental lily blooms.*

we're sitting on our fat rears in front of the television.

Herbs after Dark: Some Enchanted Evening

When hot summer days turn into hot summer nights, many of us seek refuge from the heat outdoors. We often invite friends over to the patio, fire up the grill, pop a wine cork, and crank up the stereo. Pale shafts of light from the back of the house join the warm glow of candles set in strawberry jars, which we find much more suitable for lighting the patio than for housing strawberries.

On these evenings, energy that drained away during the day starts to return. The soothing trickle of water from our pond, which abuts the patio, sets the tone for the evening (unless we've turned our stereo up too loud).

The plants surrounding us suggest a Mediterranean courtyard after dark. The brightly colored flowers and vivid green leaves fade into the darkness; gray-leaved herbs and white and pale-colored flowers glow in the soft candlelight. Moonlight makes them stand out in ghostly silhouette; even streetlights perform a kind of alchemy, turning gray to silver. Artemisias, lavenders, santolina, *Plectranthus argentatus*, licorice plant, lamb's-ears, *Verbascum bombyciferum* 'Arctic Summer', dianthus, rue, catmints— all pleasant by day—grow luminous by night.

The pale foliage of dusty miller, heliotrope, and helichrysum, subtle by day, takes on a glowing, ghostly visage by night.

The scent of many of these nocturnal beauties lingers into the evening. Variously acrid, earthy, and bracing, these smells are joined by the flowers that save their perfume for the dark, the better to attract night-flying moths. These include Oriental lilies as well as the intensely sweet-scented old-fashioned flowering tobacco. Dramatic angel's trumpet (*Datura metel*) is glorious by night, its sweet white (or sometimes dusky purple) flowers filling the air with fragrance. Some petunias, too, release a bit of the perfume after sunset, revealing their past glory before hybridizers began to value size and color over smell.

Our favorite night bloomer, however, is night-scented stock (*Matthiola longipetala* subsp. *bicornis*), a trailing annual with gray-green leaves and simple, four-petaled lavender flowers. These humble blossoms close by day and unfurl at night, releasing a euphoric fragrance rivaling that of orange blossoms and jasmine.

Sultry evenings, haunted by these unforgettable scents, linger in gardeners' minds like scenes from a Tennessee Williams play. After weeks of summer heat, we begin to long for the cooling breezes of autumn. But in the depths of winter, we find ourselves recalling the trickles of sweat on the brow, the surrounding murmur of the darkened garden, and the air heavily laden with alternating sweet and earthy scents. It stirs a longing for a season we thought would never end.

CHAPTER 5

GOING TO EXTREMES

GARDENERS CAN BE DRIVEN TO extremes by an infinite vareity of factors: culinary pleasures, explorations of traditions, nostaligic memories. The surrounding environment and limitations of a planting site can focus the gardener's attention too, as what once seemed a frustrating limitation reveals itself as newfound richness.

DRYLAND BEAUTY: HERBS OF THE DESERT

It takes many gardeners time to appreciate plants of the desert. For those who grew up around lush roses, peonies, and poppies, the lean, spare beauty of cacti and succulents seems foreign, and their spikes and barbs don't make them any friendlier. Yet these fascinating plants offer a range of form and color that rivals any other group. Their cultivation needs are generally simple, their rewards huge.

Cacti, a plant group native to the deserts of North and South America, stores water in its fat, juicy stems; the armor of spines, actually modified leaves, protects the plants from thirsty marauders. Humans have learned to circumvent these protective systems and to use the flesh and sap for folk medicine, food, even alcoholic beverages. If you subscribe to the definition of herbs as "the useful plants," cacti fit it admirably.

Succulents originated across a much broader range, including Africa. Differing from the cacti in that they store water in swollen leaves rather than stems, the succulents range from ground-huggers to tall shrubs. Both cacti and succulents offer blooms, some of which are spectacular. Under their daunting armor, a few of these plants hold a sticky but healing sap. Burn-soothing *Aloe vera* has been a fixture on kitchen windowsills about as long as cooks have been picking up hot-handled pans. This topical succulent's blue-green spikes make it a great patio plant; a number of its

An agave forms the centerpiece of this design, which also includes thyme, nasturtium, and cacti.

relatives are equally intriguing. Others hold sap of no medicinal value, and euphorbias contain a toxic, severely corrosive latex.

The long, fleshy leaves of agaves, arranged in a rosette pattern, resemble those of aloe. The leaves of *Agave parryi* are broad swords of gunmetal gray tipped with black barbs up to 1 inch long. The angular shafts of *A. victoriae-reginae* are outlined by royal silver stripes and also armed with small but yelp-inducing points. One of our favorites is *A. americana* 'Medio-picta', a variegated form whose turquoise-blue leaves sport a cream-colored band down the center. Although specimens grown outside in the desert Southwest may reach more than a yard in diameter, this form also grows hand-somely as a potted sculpture, as does the species.

The family Crassulaceae includes not only the genus *Crassula*, which includes the popular jade plant (*C. ovata*), but also such well-known succulent genera as *Aeonium*, *Dudleya*, *Echeveria*, *Kalanchoe*, *Sedum*, *Sempervivum*, and others. Each genus offers its easy-care favorites.

The so-called living stones, which belong to the genus Lithops *in the Aizoaceae, seem to have been deposited on earth by visiting aliens. They look like river stones divided in half by a deep crack.*

We especially like the pretty rosettes of members of the genera *Dudleya* and *Echeveria*, native to the deserts of the southwestern United States, Mexico, and the Andes, and *Aeonium*, which comes from North Africa and the Mediterranean. They produce attractive sprays of small, dangling flowers, but their prime attraction is their architectural shapes and vast array of foliage textures and colors. The rosette of *D. pulverulenta* eventually grows about a foot across and appears to have been sculpted from molten pewter, with showy scarlet bell-flowers as fiery accents. *A. arboreum*, native to Morocco, holds its tight, bright green rosettes on thick stems a foot or more tall, looking like something out of a Dr. Seuss book. The cultivar 'Atropurpureum' is especially dramatic with foliage the color of black raspberry jam.

The symmetrical rosettes of *Echeveria* species can be edged with reds and golds that become particularly vivid as autumn approaches, and *E.* 'Delight' has frantically frilly leaf edges. The French blue leaves of the compact *E. elegans* resemble the blossom

The startling beauty of succulents belies their ease of culture.

of an exotic rose. *E. amoena* has plump lavender leaves, while *E. setosa*'s green leaves are frosted with fine white hairs; we call it the "crystalline entity" after a space creature once featured on *Star Trek*. A hybrid called 'Mauna Loa' also has an otherworldly beauty with broad mother-of-pearl leaves shading to peach at the tips.

Clan *Kalanchoe* includes the cuddly panda plant with its felty gray leaves with brown tips. The throngs of *Sedum*, or stonecrop—there are over 400 species—include the Mexico native donkey's tail (*S. morganianum*) that begins life as an upright evergreen perennial, but spills over the side of its planter as it grows. Its delicate leaves readily detach—and readily root in whatever soil receives them—so handle this plant gently. There are so many kinds of hen-and-chickens (*Sempervivum* spp.) that it's impossible to name them; we love them for their contrasting colors, textures, and sizes as well as their persistence in forming mats of rosettes in even the poorest soils. The *Euphorbia* bunch—the spurges—is a separate and incredibly diverse family; the

Shallow terra-cotta bowls make great homes for cacti and succulents; they allow the rapid and complete drying between waterings that the plants require.

crown-of-thorns is the most prominent succulent member, but among them all the poinsettia is the most beloved.

The so-called living stones, which belong to the genus *Lithops* in the family Aizoaceae, seem to have been deposited on earth by visiting aliens. In the wild they live only in the hottest, driest areas of South Africa and Namibia; they look like river stones divided in half by a deep crack. When the odd, speckled little plants spring to life in midsummer or autumn, daisylike blossoms that are huge in comparison with the lumpy, fleshy leaves emerge from the crevices. They require such arid conditions that they must be sheltered from rain.

Pity the poor *Sansevieria trifasciata*, an African succulent known as mother-in-law's tongue. One of Rob's childhood chores was to sponge down the leaves of the mother-in-law's tongue that lurked in a corner of the living room. He resented that plant but found it fascinating. The long, dark blades of the species bear a squiggly pattern like the lines drawn by a seismograph during an earthquake. A yellow band outlines each leaf and leads to the dreaded point, which, by the way, isn't very sharp. Like many gardeners who grew up with this cliché of a houseplant, Rob always thought that mother-in-law's tongue would be one of the last things he'd ever want in the house, like Melmac dishes or swag lamps. Guess what? There's one on the sunporch, looking rather smart with variegated ivy. New cultivars, such as 'Golden Hahnii', could be added. Perhaps a shelf of Hummel figurines is next.

Succulents make ideal potted plants, both inside and out, but most are not cold-hardy. During winter, our collection lives on glass shelves in the windows of the back porch or under artificial light in the basement; in summer, they move out to the patio. They thrive with almost no care except a thorough watering every few weeks during summer, and even less in winter.

Some people mulch their pots with sand and seashells; we'd do the same, but our trips to the beach are rare.

Sharp drainage is the key to keeping potted cacti and succulents in good health. The plants may be left outside in the desert Southwest, most of the Deep South, and on most of the West Coast, but even a few degrees of frost can be deadly. Most can take full sun, but our experience indicates that they grow best in summer with some afternoon shade. Surprisingly, most of these plants put up with high humidity, as their native lands are both arid and humid. Rob trades succulents with his sister in Florida, and though the climates of Colorado and central Florida differ radically, both siblings grow gorgeous succulents.

We topdress our pots of succulents and cacti with fine gravel for both cultural and aesthetic reasons. The gravel holds moisture in the soil but not around the base of the plant as an organic mulch would; this prevents rot. Gravel also reflects light and heat, which further dries the air immediately around the plant; this benefits desert plants growing in humid or cool environs. We also think that fine beige gravel around the base of potted succulents or cacti sets off their beauty far better than bare potting soil does, especially when the perlite pieces have risen to the top like little bits of breakfast cereal. Sometimes we decorate the gravel with seashells, which also look great at the feet of Mediterranean herbs such as dittany of Crete. Some people mulch their pots with sand and seashells; we'd do the same, but our trips to the beach are rare.

Succulents are great plants for the negligent gardener. They require little fertilizer; we feed lightly several times during the summer with a standard houseplant fertilizer and not at all in winter. Succulents also shrug off high heat, acquire few pests or

Seashells top-dress pots of trailing dittany of Crete and echeverias.

diseases, and don't mind if we forget to water. A well-drained potting soil suits succulents, and they can live in small pots until thoroughly overcrowded. Most gardeners own dozens of small clay pots that dry out too quickly for geraniums, marigolds, or other summer annuals. Why not start a collection of succulents and put these pots to good use?

COLLECTING AND DISPLAYING CACTI AND SUCCULENTS

We began our desert collection by bringing home a few cuttings or small potted specimens in our carry-on bags. These days, the big cardboard box on the carousel labeled "Fragile" and "This Side Up" is stuffed with plants from nurseries that we've visited during our trip. We knock the plants out of their pots before packing, remove as much soil as possible from the roots, and wrap them in plastic and cushion them with newspaper. Bubble wrap protects succulents that may otherwise be easily damaged. We repot and prune the plants as soon as we get home; the survival rate is nearly 100 percent, which is better then we get when ordering plants by mail.

Here's how we stage our collection of

Small pots grouped together showcase the distinctive and sometimes bizarre forms and colors of cacti and succulents.

some 200 pots of desert plants to display them outdoors in the summer. First, we move them outdoors from their winter quarters. Despite their desert origins, cacti and succulents that have spent any time indoors may scald or burn when exposed to direct sunlight outdoors. We stretch shade cloth across part of the patio for a week after the danger of frost has passed to let these plants become accustomed to the bright sunshine.

We place large specimens where their ornamental qualities are seen to best advantage. Sometimes they get a prime spot on a patio table, plant stand, or garden bench. Often, we group several pots of varying sizes together to highlight the distinct rosettes and spiky leaves. We might place a pot of *Agave victoriae-reginae*, with its rich rosette of dark green and silver-rimmed leaves, to play up the frothy pale foliage of nearby potted artemisias or catmints.

Small pots of cacti on benches or flagstone tables showcase each plant's distinctive features; cacti are as varied and peculiar as their succulent cousins. Some are short and squat, others tall and distinguished, and

Do neighborhood tabbies use the cactus to scratch themselves against, or as combs for matted fur, or do they back into them during their midnight prowls?

still others mimic electrical coils, hair rollers, and prickly pencils. Some cacti bloom in winter, some in summer; the flowers, bright, shiny satin cups, are so lovely that it's hard to believe that they spring from such hostile-looking plants.

We often find patches of cat hair clinging to some of our cacti, like clues in a weird feline murder mystery. Do neighborhood tabbies use the cactus to scratch themselves against, as cows use fences, or as combs for matted fur, or do they back into them inadvertently during their midnight prowls? We'll probably never know, but removing the hair is a tiresome job.

A Sylvan Setting: Potted Herbs in Shade

"Will that grow in shade?" gardeners at Rob's talks constantly implore. We understand the problem. In our old garden, only a few square feet of ground got full sun, and the patio received only a few hours of early morning light. We experimented extensively to find interesting plants, including herbs, that would thrive in less than full sun.

Airy yarrow and brilliant portulaca draw attention to this Southwestern pot. The trough and surrounding grasses bring desert ambiance to the garden.

We now have more than one patio because we really do live outdoors in summer and enjoy more than one "room," but both are shaded. Beneath the soft, filtered light of deciduous trees, we surround ourselves with hundreds of plants that thrive with a bit more shade.

Most of our shady pots are like the ones kept in the sun—big and overstuffed. We usually start with bold foliage plants that most people associate with Victorian parlors, such as ferns, palms, dracaenas, spider plants, figs, and cast-iron plants. We accompany them with all sorts of tender herbs such as licorice plant, plectranthuses, and scented geraniums, especially those that smell of nutmeg and mint. We add perennials that could easily go in the ground but that also look smashing in pots. Lungworts are lovely as single specimens or in combinations. Comfrey—especially the striking *Symphytum ×uplandicum* 'Variegata'—becomes a showpiece rather than a background plant. Spiky rushes add height. The dwarf feverfews such as the double white *Tanacetum parthenium* 'Tom Thumb' show up better in a pot than in the garden.

*S*weet woodruff fills a whiskey half-barrel in short order and pours down its slides, looking, except for its foam of flowers, like a flat-topped boxwood cushion.

Chervil also makes a fine pot plant for us; its lacy leaves complement begonias well.

Perennial ground covers such as moneywort, pennyroyal, herb Robert, bugleweed, and barren strawberry tumble out of their pots; we like to group several kinds of these together. European wild ginger (*Asarum europaeum*) has glossy, rounded leaves that look great throughout the season; its strange brown flowers are hidden near ground level. Selfheal (*Prunella* spp.) offers attractive, dark green foliage and early-season spikes of white, pink, or lavender flowers. Dead nettle (*Lamium maculatum*) lightens up the shade with the metallic silver markings on its light green leaves. The cultivar 'White Nancy' has white flowers while those of 'Beacon Silver' and 'Pink Pewter' are pink. Lesser calamint (*Calamintha nepeta*) is a tireless summer bloomer with myriad small pink flowers. Its cousin *C. grandiflora*, sometimes known as beautiful mint, lives up to its name with showy rose-pink blossoms. Sweet woodruff fills a whiskey half-barrel in short order and pours down its sides, looking, except for its foam of flow-

The interplay of leaf color, shape, and texture are the focus of this design; the begonia blossoms give a gentle spark to catmint, coleus, apple mint, and geraniums.

ers, like a flat-topped boxwood cushion.

We don't worry much about floral pizzazz in the shady pots, relying instead on the interplay of leaf color, shape, and texture. Nevertheless, we tuck in cute little wishbone flower (*Torenia fournieri*) or a few begonias—both fibrous and tuberous—as well as a smattering of impatiens, but never in shocking pink or orange. White and pale pink ones show up nicely at twilight or when candles are lit in the evening.

Rob can't help planting dwarf Oriental lilies in the shady pots. The heady fragrance during their late summer bloom is worth the effort, and the flowers enliven the foliage arrangements for a few weeks. Last summer, a variety called 'Miss America' bloomed with such perfect, satin pink flowers that nearly every visitor touched them to see if we'd cheated by adding silk ones.

Still, the focus remains on foliage plants. Variegated forms of common herbs perform well without much direct sun. These include variegated myrtle (*Myrtus communis* 'Variegata') with cream-edged leaves and variegated black horehound (*Ballota nigra* 'Archer's Variety') with irregular white leaf markings that set off its lavender-pink flowers. Bright yellow decorates

Chervil, begonias, and lamiastrum provide a base for the huge variegated leaves of dumb cane.

Even under the shade of a silver maple, Japanese rush, pennyroyal, lady's mantle, feverfew, asparagus fern, and bronze-leaf coral bells thrive.

the green foliage of both variegated meadowsweet (*Filipendula ulmaria* 'Variegata') and variegated ginger mint (*Mentha ×gracilis* 'Variegata').

We also plant variegated forms of scented geraniums ('Atomic Snowflake', 'Prince Rupert', and 'Lady Plymouth'), strawberry, wandering Jew, doku-dami, periwinkle, Cuban oregano (*Plectranthus forsteri* 'Marginatus'), ivy, and ground ivy.

We've discovered that many "full sun" herbs also grow very well in dappled shade. Sometimes we must rotate their pots to keep them from leaning toward the sun, but we've gotten respectable performances from chives, perilla, lemongrass, lemon balm, mints, catmints, ginger, golden feverfew, rue, St.-John's-wort, and woolly thyme. Surprisingly, many succulents such as hen-and-chickens and *Aloe vera* perform better than expected in dappled shade. Our research continues.

NEW WAVE: TROPICALISMO

In horticulture, all things tropical are hot. A look of jungle exuberance is back—especially on the patio. The trend started

Cannas, once banned from tasteful gardens, are back in fashion. Companions to this striped 'Pretoria' include scented geraniums, lavender, and Cuban oregano.

several years ago and looks to continue well into the future. Top garden designers who once specialized in terribly tasteful English pastiches now cram-pack their pots with an abundance of tropical plants. Only a few years ago, most wouldn't have been caught dead with a canna or coleus on their premises, but now these plants are all the rage.

It's a rage that's more than 100 years old. The Victorians loved the lush tropical excesses of bananas, cannas, and palms. It wasn't unusual for a manicured lawn to have a circular bed of dramatic, huge-leaved castor beans or spiky clumps of New Zealand flax (*Phormium* spp.). "Carpet beds" were planted in patterns that mimicked those of the Oriental rugs that decorated fashionable Victorian floors, with the color and texture supplied by fancy-leaved geraniums, coleuses, and succulents as well as *Alternanthera ficoidea* var. *amoena*, an easily clipped dwarf herb from Central America with thin, oval leaves mottled with brown-red, orange, and purple. The way we use the plants may have changed, but these tropical wonders are as beautiful as ever.

The champion of drama, of course, is the banana tree, although our low humidity tends to singe the tips of the huge leaves, and winds may batter them.

Bold cannas look great in large terra-cotta pots. Cultivars with bronze or variegated foliage and flowers in salmon, pink, and primrose yellow are available. Dwarf varieties work especially well on small patios. The sword-shaped leaves of New Zealand flax come in bronze or stripes besides the standard dark green; an enormous clump makes an impact that few plants can rival. Ginger and cardamom, both with lustrous straplike leaves, also make handsome potted specimens.

A castor bean plant makes a riveting centerpiece for a large pot, even if it doesn't attain the stature that it might in the ground. Who needs a 20-foot castor bean tree on the patio, anyway? Take care, however, if children are present; these plants, and especially the seed, are toxic.

The champion of drama, of course, is the banana tree. The only drawback to growing one where we live is that the low humidity tends to singe the leaf tips, and high winds may batter the enormous leaves. Lack of humidity and cool nights also tend to slow the growth of taro or elephant's-ear (*Colo-*

Cannas, nasturtiums, and coleus signal the renewed popularity of all things tropical.

casia esculenta), but it's still worth the effort to keep the beast fed and watered to produce glossy green leaves up to 2 feet long and 1 foot wide. New varieties feature purple-black leaves or bold maroon veining. Grow them in a pond or glazed pot with no drainage hole for best results. These and other tropical herbs, such as gotu kola and kava-kava (*Piper methysticum*), sulk in cool temperatures, and they hate icy irrigation water. A friend funnels rainwater from her gutters into a barrel and uses it to water her container plants in the belief that the luke-warm water helps ginger, bananas, and taro grow more vigorously.

Tubs of oleanders also hark back to the golden age of tropical splendor. These shrubs bear clusters of sweetly scented pink, peach, or white blossoms above shiny oval leaves; we remember huge specimens that surrounded the carousel at Elitch's Gardens in Denver. Although all parts of the plant contain very poisonous cardioactive glycosides similar to those found in foxglove (*Digitalis* spp.), we've never heard of a child eating any at the old Victorian

Potted herbs and perennials surround and are even sunk into this pond.

theme park, but parents of young children might best skip growing them.

All sorts of palms, from the amusing ponytail palm to the never-say-die parlor palm, may be easily accommodated on the patio. Tropical flowering herbs complement these as well as other bold foliage plants. Many tender species of *Salvia*, such as pineapple sage, Mexican bush sage, *S. greggii*, and Texas sage revel in hot, humid weather. African lion's-ear (*Leonotis leonurus*) produces its whorls of hairy orange flowers after a long heat wave. Zinnias, dahlias, and marigolds—all originally from Mexico—also thrive in torrid weather. Mexican mint marigold (*Tagetes lucida*), noted for its sweet-smelling leaves and small yellow flowers, won't even bother to grow unless it gets good and hot.

Other companions for bold tropical herbs include the newly respectable coleuses, perilla, feverfews, scented geraniums, plectranthuses, spider plants, bromeliads, variegated ivies, wandering Jew, dead nettle, and cast-iron plant. Common houseplants such as mother-in-law's tongue or dracaena look suddenly important when they're positioned on a shady patio in the company of flowering begonias and impatiens. Queen Victoria might feel right at home.

Though we haven't actually scoured any pots with the horsetail, we know that if Martha Stewart were stopping by for a visit, we could.

STILL WATERS:
AQUATIC HERBS
IN POTS

Ponds can be a real joy—we love our goldfish even if we haven't gotten to the point of hand-feeding and petting them. We also like experimenting with aquatic plants. One summer we tried the swamp look, stuffing the pond so full of plants that eventually we had to pull them aside just to feed the fish. An explosion of water hyacinths was the main problem; it clogged our pond, just as it has clogged the waterways of the South. We've recently seen patio furniture with the backs and seats woven from dried water hyacinths. This is progress, and it also means that under our broad definition, water hyacinth is now an official herb, that is, a useful plant.

Other useful plants that have populated our pond include rushes, cattails, horsetails, papyrus, lotus, watercress, doku-dami, elephant's-ear, irises, marsh marigold, water mint (*Mentha aquatica*), marsh pennywort (*Hydrocotyle vulgaris*), and water agrimony (*Bidens tripartita*). We've used the rushes and cattails in wreaths and arrangements, and though we haven't actually scoured any pots with the horsetail, we know that if Martha Stewart were stopping by for a visit, we could.

We also make small water gardens in containers. They're not nearly as much work as the pond, which has a pump and filter that need periodic cleaning, occasionally leak, and regularly get rearranged by raccoons. The trick to achieving a balanced little "pond" is to include a few surface leaves to block some of the sunlight, limit algae growth, and shelter the fish; some rooted plants that will use up nutrients and limit algae; and fish to feed upon the algae. A few small goldfish in each container also keep the water-filled pots from becoming mosquito nurseries.

The smaller water gardens also enable us to grow more aquatic herbs. We use some large blue-and-white porcelain fishbowls, purchased years ago at an import shop, filled with a few potted plants of dokudami, variegated rush (*Juncus effusus*

Our miniature water gardens are housed in these old porcelain pots; families of goldfish live there happily, too.

Potted bamboo is a pleasure, associating benignly with pink Nerine bowdenii, *ivy, oxalis, scented geraniums, alstromeria, and the giant leaves of a philodendron.*

HERBS IN POTS

'Aureus Striatus' or 'Zabrinus', and some floating water lettuce (*Pistia stratiotes*), all accented by colored glass Japanese fishermen's floats. Any glazed or terracotta pot can be turned into a tiny pond. Plug the drainage hole with epoxy or plumber's caulk. Except for those that must float, such as water lettuce, the plants stay in their pots, propped up as necessary on cement blocks, bricks, or stacks of plastic nursery pots. To bring one of these small water gardens indoors for the winter, first dump out most of the water. Refill it when you've placed it where it will stay until warm weather returns.

DOING THYME: THE INCARCERATED HERB

Some herbs are outright thugs: they overwhelm, invade, and refuse eviction without drastic steps such as air strikes. In most regions of the country, comfrey, lemon balm, tansy, Roman wormwood, western mugwort, sweet woodruff, bishop's weed, most bamboos, horseradish, and most mints shouldn't be unleashed in a civilized garden. These herbs sometimes make

Sometimes, just for fun, we force gardener's-garters, bishop's weed, or variegated ground ivy to share a half-barrel with another herbal felon.

great plants for tough spots, but giving them the slightest break can turn them into garden monsters. Give them an inch, and they'll take a county.

Imprison these invasive herbs in suitable containers, and the world's suddenly a better place. A good many become handsome specimens. Take variegated horseradish (*Armoracia rusticana*) 'Variegata'); its irregular white streaks on broad, frilly leaves put pizzazz in a prime spot, but you don't want it everywhere.

Other herbal hooligans become class acts when their bad habits are curtailed. A wooden half-barrel turns into a suitable, long-term home for 'Silver King' or 'Valerie Finnis' artemisias, both noted for running roughshod over their neighbors. Sometimes—just for fun—we force gardener's-garters, bishop's weed, or variegated ground ivy to share a half-barrel with another herbal felon. The results are often striking, even though the effect may vary from year to year as the inmates duke it out. Occasionally, one wins.

Variegated ground ivy has never been allowed a foothold in our garden, but it's wonderful spilling out of a pot or hanging baskets. The long tendrils of scalloped round leaves with distinctive white edges must not be allowed to touch the soil below, however, or they'll hit the ground running. Dead nettle and periwinkle will also try to escape their Alcatraz pots, but, depending on your garden conditions, are usually easier to control.

It's difficult to generalize about the invasiveness of particular herbs because climate and culture play an enormous part in turning an otherwise meek herb into a garden-gobbling beast, and vice versa. Some herbs behave perfectly for several years; only later does the gardener discover that the ingrates have been secretly installing a world invasion force below ground: marsh woundwort (*Stachys palustris*) pulled this trick on us.

On the other hand, we've been repeatedly warned about the aggressiveness of doku-dami (*Houttuynia cordata*). After killing three plants, we planted one more in a pot, not to control it but to keep it alive. Our dry climate and notorious stinginess with water can be blamed for our failure with this Oriental culinary herb; some gar-

deners grow it in plastic pots sunk in a pond, where it thrives but can't escape.

Some herbs can be incarcerated without just cause. There's usually no need to lock up thyme, creeping golden oregano, dune silver (*Artemisia stelleriana*), or moneywort, but they look great as solitary specimens, filling and cascading from a bulky container or elegant urn. We took rusty metal truck wheels—abandoned in our alley—and rolled them to positions of prominence on either side of a grape arbor. Filled with soil and planted with no-fuss hen-and-chickens, they nearly overflowed in a single season. They visually anchor the arbor, contrasting with the airy harebells and dianthuses congregating around their bases.

Many tough perennials may be left in large containers almost indefinitely. Others benefit from periodic rejuvenation; we dig up small clumps of the plant, discard the rest along with the old soil, and replant the good parts in fresh soil. Many perennial herbs survive the winter in large pots without protection, but those that are only marginally hardy may die if the winter is especially harsh. Losing them usually doesn't

Many perennial herbs survive the winter in large pots without protection, but those that are only marginally hardy may die if the winter is harsh.

present a huge problem: your neighbor may just have a giant patch of mint or tansy from which they can spare a new start.

Dream Vacation: A Summer Break for Houseplants

Every year, we see this happen: People think their spindly, leaf-dropping, spider mite-infested houseplants need some sun and tote them outside one morning to "catch some rays." By lunchtime, the plants are incinerated. The reason that many houseplants survive indoors is that they don't require direct sunlight. Their native habitat is the forest floor, where light is filtered by a canopy of trees above. Other houseplants, such as succulents, thrive in our homes because of low water and humidity requirements. Many appreciate bright light but must be gradually reintroduced to the full force of the sun's rays after a winter under glass.

In the past, we ignored our houseplants in summer, leaving a windowsill of pitiful, unwatered ferns and spider plants in the laundry room. Then we figured out how a little summer vacation improved these plants, so now they go outdoors when we do. We don't haphazardly deposit them under a tree and hope the sprinkler will reach them—no, we give our plants a dream vacation.

Houseplants can offer 365 days of plea-sure. They can be integrated into container displays on terraces, porches, and decks. Some are suitable for a sunny patio, while others thrive in shady sites. With a little creativity in arranging them, they can play starring roles wherever they grow.

The east side of our house features an interplay of foliage textures of shade-loving perennials. This garden frames a circular lawn 20 feet in diameter. The lawn cried out for a central focal point, but we resisted the urge to plunk a concrete cherub in the middle. Instead, we carved out a 4-foot circle in the center and filled it with pots of houseplants, including herbs.

A variegated spider plant (*Chlorophytum comosum*) spills like a waterfall from an urn in the middle. Beneath its arching runners, we've grouped variegated Cuban oregano, Japanese rush (*Acorus graminifolia*), flowering maple, doku-dami, dracaena, and ivy along with green-foliaged ferns, clivia, golden moneywort, and chartreuse coleus. The subtle combinations emphasize the tranquility of the garden.

Common houseplants that are suitable for a shady foliage composition include many old favorites. Among the large-leaved plants to add structure to an outdoor grouping are philodendrons, dumb cane, peace lily, Chinese evergreen, cast-iron plant, large dracaenas, and palms. For contrast, the smaller leaves of jade plant, creeping fig, and peperomia are effective.

Trailing houseplants such as hoya, pothos, asparagus fern, grape ivy, or lotus vine can be displayed from atop a pedestal or in a basket hung from a tree branch or arbor.

A site with bright dappled shade, perhaps under a tiny-leaved honey locust tree, will support all of these plants. Trees or shelters that cast dense shade, however, will support only the stalwart philodendrons, peace lily, and other classic low-light houseplants.

The patio on the south side of our house dazzles in sunshine. Here, houseplants contribute interesting foliage that complements colorful annual flowers. We grow dozens of kinds of scented geraniums, all with handsome leaves and each with a distinct fragrance. Except for a few clipped standards, we prune these plants vigorously when they go outside so that they form dense little bushes.

Fancy-leaved geraniums intrigue us as much as their scented cousins. They may have had their heyday during the Victorian era, but they deserve a place in the contemporary garden. The foliage looks much like that of ordinary garden geraniums with one important difference: it's striped with one or more colors— white, yellow, burnt orange, gold, maroon. The flowers of fancy-leaved types, like those of the the scenteds, take a back seat to the leaves.

Both kinds of geraniums can be displayed in groupings of separate pots or in larger pots with summer annuals. We like the green-white-red-leaved 'Italian Skies', with scarlet blossoms. 'Mrs. Henry Cox' is similar but produces pink flowers. We like to combine a few plants of either variety in a big cast-iron urn with spike dracaena, flowering tobacco, lobelia (*Lobelia erinus*), and asparagus ferns. This strategy ties that area of the patio together visually, much like using several complementary patterns of fabric on throw pillows scattered throughout a room.

Other small houseplants that root easily from cuttings and perform well in patio containers include purple heart, many kinds of wandering Jew, and Cuban oregano. The latter, a relative of Swedish ivy, is noted for its rounded, white-edged leaves on trailing stems.

Our eclectic collection of potted plants enriches the outdoor living areas, just as it brings life to the house in winter. We sometimes become so accustomed to a palm or spider plant indoors that we forget to appreciate its beauty. Placing it in a new setting stirs creativity and opens our eyes. If we can't take a dream vacation to the tropical lands where our houseplants grow wild, we've come pretty close to getting the effect at home.

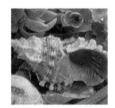

CHAPTER 6
THE GREAT INDOORS

IN WINTER, IT SEEMS THAT WE SIMPLY HAVE too many plants. If we limited our indoor tenants to a couple of dozen, winter wouldn't be such an ordeal, but we bring in a couple of hundred plants. So we envy people with greenhouses. They might complain about the work involved—maintenance, pests, heating and cooling problems, not to mention the initial expense—but we envy them nevertheless. Everything we grow is under lights or next to a window, not at all ideal.

A greenhouse makes winter easy on herbs that must come indoors. It's humid and bright, although the shorter days, winter clouds, and the low position of the sun and the diminished strength of its rays affect plant performance. For many greenhouse plants, growth stalls, flowering diminishes or ceases, and stems become weak or spindly. Multiply those problems by ten, and you've got the picture inside an ordinary house or apartment with a few south or west-facing windows. Face it: most herbs are going to look terrible under these conditions.

Plants growing in the house have to put up with conditions that are comfortable for people, but not helpful to plants. Leaves yellow and drop, stems lean for the light, and new leaves are pale and small. Spider mites, aphids, and mealy bugs move in. It's a mess, but one with a purpose. The enforced winter rest is good for most plants, and for people too.

We don't want the household spider population to rest, however. We count on them, cobwebs notwithstanding, to keep the aphids, spider mites, and whiteflies in check. People with arachnophobia could never live in our house; just visiting might provoke a seizure of terror.

We really regret not owning a greenhouse at watering time. We line up the watering cans at the kitchen sink, leaving the tap running in one can while racing around the house with another one, trying to make it back to the kitchen before the can there overflows. Appropriately frantic music (it's great to garden to music) for this is "The Saber Dance" or "Flight of the Bumblebee."

If we had a greenhouse, we could just turn on a hose without worrying about water stains on the hardwood floors. We have no water source in the basement, where many herbs spend the winter under florescent lights and where we strike cuttings and start seedlings. It's an adventure to navigate the basement stairs with heavy watering cans, ducking to avoid head bonks, without spilling half the water along the way.

There are ways to streamline watering, such as using hoses that attach to the sink faucet. Several so-called self-watering devices are also available, including a useful tray with wicks that would be handy if travel prevents you from checking your plants regularly. You can make your own version of this watering system by placing a small piece of new lamp wick in the bottom of a terra-cotta pot and setting the pot in a cache pot. Be sure that the inner pot does not actually sit in the water to prevent the plant from drowning.

Every few weeks we get out scissors and plastic bags to do a little grooming and sometimes use the fine nozzle on the vacuum cleaner to pick up the debris. During winter most of the plants experience benign neglect, remaining on the dry side and going without fertilizer—another way to encourage the plants to rest. Although some herbs stay attractive throughout winter captivity, most look dreadful. As soon as spring comes and they're set back outside, repotted, fertilized, and pruned, they'll regain their former glory.

Don't stress out if your herbs appear tatty in the depths of winter—it's not permanent. Don't overwater and certainly don't pump them up with fertilizer. Be patient, for the longer days of spring will reinvigorate them.

About two months before we can set the plants back outside, we give haircuts, increase water, and pay a bit more attention to pest problems. Most of the pests, and certainly whiteflies, should be wiped out before the plants return to the garden. After serious inspection, we spray the

Don't stress out if your herbs appear tatty in the depths of winter—it's not permanent. Be patient, for the longer days of spring will invigorate them.

To start seeds and cuttings indoors, a bank of fluorescent lights is necessary.
We use the cool white bulbs by the case and have great success with them.

undersides of leaves with soap again and again over several weeks to eliminate whiteflies as they hatch. We use cotton swabs soaked in rubbing alcohol to dab away mealybugs, and light oil sprays to smother individual pests that lodge in impenetrable crevices. Ladybugs begin to hatch inside in February and March and start to gobble up aphids. Any really badly infested plants get thrown in the dumpster—it happens.

Under Lights: Herbal Propagation

Some novice gardeners think they need a lovely "set" of lights and trays to grow things. We'd like that too—we'll get it when we build our picturesque Victorian greenhouse with soil in antique wooden bins and hand-made wooden flats for sowing seeds and piped-in Vivaldi.

In reality, we spread an old sheet on the living room floor. We use a coffee can to fill our recycled plastic six packs with store-bought seed starter-mix and stack the trays as we go. One of us invariably gets distracted by an old movie and falls asleep on the couch. Refreshed from the nap, he gets the job of making labels for each packet of seeds before we sow them; we learned years ago that it's easy to get them mixed up. We turn the heat way down so our hands don't sweat as we handle the seeds between a thumb and fore-

finger. It's a thrilling afternoon all the way around, punctuated by Rob's timeless renditions of "Strangers in the Night" and "Guantanamera." The tragic part is that Rob doesn't know the words, so he just sings, "Guantanamera, da da da Guantanamera" over and over.

When the sowing is done, we water the flats in the kitchen, cover them with clear plastic domes, and haul them down to the basement, where our random collection of old fluorescent shop lights hangs from the ceiling beams. After setting the flats on "tables" of old hollow-core doors, we lower the lights to just above the domes. A timer assures that the flats will get sixteen hours of light daily.

This low-tech rig isn't pretty, but it works. After studying literature on the light spectrum of various fluorescent bulb types, we decided to ignore it. Several years of experimenting with different types of lights showed that seedlings grow toward the cheaper, cool-white florescent bulbs and away from other types of bulbs. Now we buy the cheapest florescent bulbs we can find—by the case.

When seedlings sprout, we remove the covers. The plant room's temperature stays at about 60°F, promoting slow, stocky growth. With luck, more than one seedling germinates in each cell; we thin them with tweezers or fingernails. We take up a pickle fork to transplant a few if blank cells occurs in a six-pack, but the extra basil plants are usually eaten on the spot.

Our mistakes have taught us plenty. For instance, starting some seeds too early—basil, parsley, and nasturtium, to name a few—produces leggy and root-bound plants. Other seeds, however, require a longer period of growth to reach transplant size; these include lavender, mealy cup sage (*Salvia farinacea*), and golden feverfew.

We start cuttings of plants nearly all year long. There seems to be a long tradition among gardeners of surreptitiously pinching plants in other people's gardens to start new ones—not that we would ever do such a thing or encourage others to do so. All you have to do in our garden is ask. Striking cuttings is a good skill to have for rooting a

THE METER READER'S TALE

The meter reader risks life and limb negotiating her way to the basement. She must wend her way down the stairs past pots, buckets, and boxes of seeds. "Store in a cool, dry, dark place," advise the seed packets—what better place than on the stairs to the basement? Then she faces the plant room's tangle of extension cords, timers, and makeshift tables that hold the flats of seedlings.

Perhaps if the meter reader saw something she could recognize, maybe an African violet, it would ease her mind. We can imagine her stories about Rob, told to her fellow meter readers:

This guy is always in the same gray sweat pants, and there's filthy

sheets all over the living room floor. He hasn't cleaned that basement

since the dawn of time, and I have no idea what he's growing down in

his laboratory. And wait 'til you here this: When I left the house, I

could here him singing "La Bamba"! I just about barfed. He's supposed

to be some kind of writer or something, but I'm tellin' ya—this guy is

a taco short of a combination platter.

newly acquired treasure or increasing your stock of plants.

Cuttings of some plants, especially woody ones, require special treatment such as layering, which is burying a stem in the ground to allow it to root, but many will take root if stuck in soil. We often save cuttings of container plants to avoid keeping the whole plant through the winter. As winter draws to a close, we take a look at the plants kept in the house to decide which ones are due for a trim, and which ones we want to increase for next summer's containers.

Late winter is a good time to start new cuttings of tender lavender and salvia cultivars and species, as well as begonia, coleus, helichrysum, plectranthus, and succulents. Scented, fancy-leaf, and zonal geraniums, flowering maple (*Abutilon* spp.), sweet potato vines, wandering Jew, and purple-heart (*Setcreasea pallida*, also known as *Tradescantia pallida*), grow well from cuttings.

We take cuttings at least 3 to 4 inches long and strip off most of the leaves except a few at the top. Cuttings with more leaves often do poorly because they lack a root system to support the top growth.

Nearly all cuttings benefit from a hardening-off period to let the wound at the base of the stem form a callous, thus preventing rot. Left in a cool place, most plants keep overnight before wilting, and many hold for several days.

Then we recommend brushing the bottom of the stem and the nubs where the leaves once were with a rooting hormone because roots form on many plants at these former leaf axils. The compound, which contains antibacterials, looks like talcum powder and is easily brushed on with a watercolor brush. We cover new cuttings with clear plastic covers and keep them in a warm place out of direct sun.

A good rooting mixture is equal parts sterile potting soil, sharp sand, and vermiculite or perlite, although we use whatever sterile potting soil we have on hand. Firm the soil around the cutting to be sure that it contacts the stem, then water the cuttings thoroughly from the bottom. Rooting often begins in about ten days, but as long

A good rooting mixture is equal parts sterile potting soil, sharp sand, and vermiculite or perlite, but we use sterile potting soil we have on hand.

as the foliage stays green on the stem, there's hope. We often give foliar fertilizer to cuttings to speed up rooting.

Some plants root best when warmed from the bottom. For this we use a propagation mat, which is basically an electric blanket without fleece that can be rolled out, plugged in, and covered with flats of cuttings. A temperature of about 80°F is about right for quick rooting. Some propagation mats feature thermostats, but our vintage second-hand mat doesn't, so it has cooked several batches of cuttings. As a precaution, we now prop flats to raise them several inches above the mat and keep an eye on the soil to make sure it stays moist.

PARADISE BY THE PACKET

Seed companies count on our winter frustrations to keep them in business, knowing that we'll take a chance on par-

Seeds are the best bargain in horticulture; shop the seed catalogs carefully for herb varieties that you won't find in your local garden center.

Rob Goes to Seed

Every winter I sort through a mishmash of seeds stored in shoeboxes in my office closet. It's dark and dry in there, so many seeds remain viable for several years. Going through the packets is a trip down memory lane as I recall last year's butter-yellow nasturtiums, salmon-pink flowering tobacco, purple-leaf basil, and over-productive squash. Foraging through the boxes helps me recall the late sun illuminating borders brimming with flowers, and I can almost smell the bacon, lettuce, and tomato sandwiches that go hand-in-hand with a warm summer evening.

Not every thought is about the past, however, because the boxes hold packets promising future memories. The apricot-colored foxgloves that I sowed last year will bloom this spring. I'm looking forward to new species of *Campanula*, *Allium*, *Digitalis*, and *Verbascum*. Throughout our garden, young perennial seedlings wait to strut their stuff as the season progresses.

Is it any wonder that I impatiently wait for the mail carrier's footsteps each day? It's a wonderful time when all those catalogs start arriving. Generations of American gardeners have kept their sanity during tough winters with the help of seed catalogs. The wind may howl outside and snow stack up on the porch, but spring waits in the stacks of catalogs piled on the coffee table. I'd rather curl up with a pile of them than the latest potboiler from Danielle Steele. (Frankly, I'd rather curl up with a wolverine than one of her novels, but that's a matter of taste.)

Catalogs are fun. Some are cleverly written, some show pretty pictures, and others offer odd tidbits of information, gardening tips, and even recipes. A catalog is also the horticultural equivalent of a long, hot bath that washes away present reality and transplants us to a golden, sunny day. It makes us dream about all that we can accomplish, the wonders we can coax from the soil, and the pleasures that will soon return.

adise at a buck-fifty a packet. Some gardeners, like me, are easy targets. They know that I will order too much, my check's in the mail, and if necessary I will sell my sofa to finance my seed orders, but competition between companies helps keep prices down. A packet of seeds is the best buy in horticulture.

Aside from the obvious savings of raising your own plants, there are many advantages to shopping for seeds by mail. Today's seed companies fall into two categories: the generalists and the specialists. Catalogs from the generalists offer a mixed bag of annuals, vegetables, herbs, and perennials. They'll trumpet new introductions— usually improved varieties of old standbys like petunias, impatiens, tomatoes, lettuce, and corn. The companies have put a great effort into finding varieties that perform well throughout much of the country and demonstrate advances in vigor and disease resistance.

The specialist catalogs cater to gardeners with particular interests or growing conditions. Some feature heirloom flowers, herbs, and vegetables, flowers for cutting and drying, wild flowers, high-altitude plants, gourmet vegetables, or plants that fit particular niches, such as rock gardens or meadows.

Many dedicated seed growers ignore the catalog offerings that will likely appear at their local garden centers and roadside markets in the spring. Why waste premium growing space in your home greenhouse, sun porch, or fluorescent light garden on common annuals, herbs, and vegetables that are sprouting in six-packs just down the road? Abundant, reasonably priced petunias, marigolds, impatiens, dusty miller, lobelia, snapdragons, sweet alyssum, green basil, peppers, cabbage, and most popular varieties of tomatoes may not be worth the effort it takes to grow them from seed.

I order seeds for plants that rarely turn up at local greenhouses and must be direct-sown to grow well—larkspur, annual poppies, bachelor buttons, cosmos, nigella.

I order seeds for plants that rarely turn up at local greenhouses and must be direct-sown to grow well—larkspur, annual poppies, bachelor buttons, cosmos, nigella. They generally resist being regimented into six-packs. Beans, peas, corn, beets, carrots, dill, and fennel fall into this category as well.

Ordering seeds by mail also makes sense for those with a taste for the exotic. For example, some catalogs offer a dozen or more varieties of basil; we try to sample a few each season. Heirloom vegetables also fascinate some gardeners, although few have impressed us enough to turn into heirlooms around here.

Flower lovers may find that catalogs offer favorites in single colors, when generally only mixed colors are found. General catalogs have turned to offering only mixed colors of zinnias, cosmos, China asters, portulaca, statice, strawflowers, gomphrena, flowering tobacco, morning glories, larkspur, hollyhocks, and many others. Specialist catalogs, on the other hand, can cater to gardeners who prefer separate flower colors.

Regional catalogs serve gardeners who face hazards such as short growing seasons and generally cool summers. Some emphasize vegetables that mature quickly, but buyers should not get too carried away by pretty pictures or promises. If you have a short growing season, check the maturation dates of the seeds you'd like to order. There's no point in growing a melon that will ripen a week after your first snowfall.

Compare prices, but don't let that be your first consideration. Blue bachelor buttons may be two bits cheaper than the pink or maroon ones, but order what you really want. I cross-check my "want lists" from each catalog and usually go with the cheapest. On the other hand, I've found that some companies are more generous than others. Packets from some suppliers are stuffed with hundreds of seeds, while others seem mighty stingy. I've torn packets apart to find that last seed or two that stuck in the folds. I've sat in the kitchen looking at a few almost-invisible specks and asked out loud, "Is that all there is?" These companies go down to the bottom of my list.

Most companies that I deal with should be commended for their prompt service. It's not unusual to receive an order within a week. I order as early as possible to ensure that seeds I've got my heart set on aren't sold out, but occasionally I'm disappointed. A few companies have bad reputations for not delivering what they promise; they earned them by sending out half-filled orders accompanied by credit slips or refunds. I prefer refund checks, since the credit slips seem to quickly disappear. I've never cashed one in; my theory is that they're printed on paper that decomposes in my desk drawer during the summer.

Be realistic about how much space you have indoors to grow seeds. I am not—I order way too much, so my shoeboxes always contain a dozen or so packets that I didn't have the space to sow the previous season. Yet I don't regret ordering too much—it's a small price to pay for making it through the winter.

END OF SEASON: PLAYING GOD

Emptying pots at the end of the season takes time—anyone crazy enough to grow 600 pots of plants must eventually face this reality. The back porch is full, we can barely see out of the south and west-facing windows, and fluorescent lights in the basement illuminate a hodgepodge of potted herbs and tropical plants unhappy about the end of their summer vacation. The dark basement storage room houses pots of dormant agapanthus, alstroemeria, cannas, lilies, and oxalis. We've run out of room.

About 300 pots of plants don't make the final cut, which makes it sound like we think this whole thing out. We don't. The so-called final cut is usually made during a snowstorm or on that fateful night when the TV weatherman announces that the first hard freeze is upon us. It's really annoying when this happens in September.

Plants that don't get moved hastily inside must face the frost. Some are annuals with predetermined fates; there's little point in saving them. Others are tender tropicals that failed to meet expectations or had worn out their welcome in the garden. One and all, these plants surrender to the cold.

THE HERBS IN ROB'S OFFICE

My office isn't normal. It's at home for one thing, which isn't that unusual these days, but I've made it a comfortable place to work. This former spare bedroom could be mistaken for a living room (albeit a messy one) with its wingback chairs, oak-topped white wicker table, a china cabinet that holds slides and books, and an Oriental carpet underfoot.

The walls are the deepest imaginable shade of blue. I've never bought into the conventional school of thought that white paint makes a room look larger. Quite the contrary, my walls stretch out like an infinite night sky. On the walls hang favorite Broadway show posters and covers from *The Herb Companion*. One window looks north out over the front porch to the front garden, while the other, nearest my chair, overlooks the shady garden. In the summer, I can open it to hear the soothing gurgle of the irrigation ditch that runs through the corner of our property. Plants line the windowsills.

Few people would choose such an environment in which to work, but it suits me. I couldn't change places with most of my friends who work in actual office buildings. Most of them inhabit sunless cubicles that no amount of family photos, calendars, and knickknacks can cheer up.

It's criminal to force people to live without windows. In the 1960s and 1970s, I attended "modern" schools that had no windows. Perhaps the architects thought that the distraction of sunshine or snow would keep students from daydreaming and keep our minds on our studies. All it did was to give me headaches—probably from the fluorescent lights—and motivate me ditch class as often as possible. Surely I would have passed geometry if there'd been a couple windows in that room (and if I hadn't got caught cheating on a test).

People who work in windowless environments should strike or quit or at least add a grow light to their cubicle. Spider plants, cast-iron plants, and philodendrons are better than nothing, especially if they get a pretty pot and a bath once in awhile. A grow light makes it possible to grow some favorite herbs in the office, and people with actual windows can grow all sorts of things. It's possible to grow a few culinary herbs, such as basil, to liven up a plastic-encased deli salad or tuna sandwich.

The trick to growing herbs in the office (including mine) is to consider most of them to be temporary employees. With the low light of winter or office lighting and the even lower indoor humidity, few herbs will achieve long-term performance. Eventually they start to decline and can be brought home for rejuvenation (if a better environment for them exists there) or thrown on the compost pile after their tour of duty.

Herbs with high light requirements, such as lavender, thyme, and santolina, don't last long in most offices. I suspect most people overwater office plants, anyway. Even in the depths of winter, however, such delightful plants as scented geraniums, Cuban oregano, and dwarf citrus trees may last for months.

A friend of mine is lucky enough to work in an office with spacious, south-facing windows. She grows lots of herbs on her windowsill. Even her rosemary grows—mine regularly commit suicide—even if it gets a bit scraggly in midwinter. Her santolina and scented geraniums usually need a haircut, just as mine do, and I've noticed a few brown leaves clustered like little dust bunnies beneath the plants. In my office, these dust bunnies are more like dust elephants.

My friend brings in temporary recruits, just as I do. Amaryllis, cyclamen, freesias, and forced paperwhites add color and fragrance. Orchids manage passably well on the north windowsill of my office; I'll bet they'd like my friend's window even better. Maybe I'll haul my worst specimens to her office to see if she can work some magic with them.

Nobody sees the casualties of my home office, but in a real office everybody witnesses the gradual decline of potted plants. By interjecting new plants and making the fading ones disappear, your coworkers will think that you not only read *The Herb Companion* regularly, but that you should probably write for it.

INDEX

Italic page numbers indicate photographs.

E

echeveria 152
Euphorbia 128, 149–150
evening pots 141–142

F

fancy-leaf geranium *40*, 99
fennel *66*
fenugreek *66*
fertilizer 45–46
feverfew *159*
flowering maple *34, 126*
flowering tobacco *52*
Foeniculum vulgare 66
fountain grass *73*
fuchsia *122*

G

'Garden Party' lily *102*
garlic chives 75
gazpacho 81–83
   recipe 82
geranium *25, 126, 130, 157*
geraniums, scented 67–68
golden marjoram 40
Greek spitting cucumber 30
greenhouses 174–175

H

hanging baskets 123–124
healing herbs 16
Helichrysum 'Limelight' *101*
helichrysum *141*
heliotrope *141*
hen-and-chickens *133*, 149
herbal propagation 177–184
   catalogs 182–183
      ordering seeds 182
      rooting cuttings 178–180
      sowing seeds 180–183
herbs for sweets 90
herbs in the office 185–186
horehound 68
hypertufa 29–31
hyssop 68
Hyssopus officinalis 68

I

impatiens 122, 130
indoor herbs 173–186
insects 46–53
invasive herbs 167–169
Italian cooking 83–85
Italian parsley 65
ivy *14, 101, 130, 166*

rue 99, 140

Rumex spp. 76–77

topiaries 15, 116–121

trash cans 31

Trigonella foenum-graecum 66

Tropaeolum majus 72

tropical herbs 17, 159–164

trowel 32

turkey casserole, recipe 88

V

variegated myrtle *101*

Verbena patagonica 86

Verbena rigida 37

W

water breaker 33

water gardens 165–167

watering accessories 33

watering 42–45
  drip systems 42
  dry mulch 43
  hand watering 43
  overwatering 43
  wet mulch 45

whiteflies 50–51

window boxes 15, 125–133
  attracting butterflies and hummingbirds 127
  building 123
  care 131
  seasonal 127
  suitable flowers 129
  tips for 131

Y

yarrow *155*

More Gardening Books

From Interweave Press

Herbs in the Garden
The Art of Intermingling
Rob Proctor and David Macke

These two creative designers suggest a bounty of ideas for using herbs in your garden: from borders to footpaths, from background walls to terrace and patio displays. All are reflected in Rob's beautiful photographs.

From the authors of Herbs in Pots!

Hardbound, $29.95 U.S./$39.95 Canada plus shipping and handling

Basil
An Herb Lover's Guide

Thomas DeBaggio and
Susan Belsinger

This comprehensive guide is a growing/cooking double-feature! Instructions for growing basil are included, along with a profile of Forty-five popular varieties. The thirty-six basil recipes are enhanced by glorious full-color photos.

Paperback, $19.95 U.S.
$29.95 Canada plus shipping & handling

Growing Herbs from Seed, Cutting, and Root
An Adventure in Small Miracles

Thomas DeBaggio

The author shatters common myths, advances new techniques, and offers ideas essential for creating healthy, vigorous plant starts for the herb garden. An abundance of photographs ensures success every step of the way.

Paperback, $9.95 U.S.
$14.95 Canada plus
shipping & handling